WHAT DOES THE BIBLE SAY ABOUT SUICIDE?

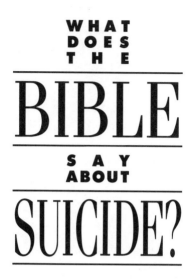

WHAT DOES THE BIBLE SAY ABOUT SUICIDE?

James T. Clemons

Fortress Press   **Minneapolis**

WHAT DOES THE BIBLE SAY ABOUT SUICIDE?

Scripture quotations unless otherwise noted are from the Revised Standard Version of the Bible, copyright © 1946, 1952, and 1971 by the Division of Christian Education of the National Council of Churches.

Cover design: Pollock Design Group
Typesetting: Peregrine Publications

Library of Congress Cataloging-in-Publication Data
Clemons, James T.
    What does the Bible say about suicide? / James T. Clemons.
      p. cm.
    Bibliography: p.
    ISBN 0-8006-2399-1
    1. Suicide—Biblical teaching. 2. Suicide—Religious aspects—Christianity. I. Title.
BS680.S855C55 1990
241'.697—dc20   89-35701
                                                CIP

The paper used in this publication meets the minimum requirements of American National Standard for Information Sciences—Permanence of Paper for Printed Library Materials, ANSI Z329.48-1984.

Manufactured in the U.S.A.   AF 1-2399

94   93   92   91   90   1   2   3   4   5   6   7   8   9   10

Contents

Preface

Suicide is now ranked the eighth leading cause of death in American society.[1] Not only among teenagers, to whom so much media attention has been given, or among the elderly, where the highest rate is to be found among white males, but also among other groups as well, suicide has become a serious problem. Women, children, ethnic minorities (especially black males), and military personnel are among those to whom suicidologists have given special attention.

The federal government has addressed the issue of youth suicide through a task force established by the Department of Health and Human Services. In 1989, it published a four-volume report of research and recommendations based on four years of intense study by the nation's leading professionals in the field of suicidology. Some states have their own Youth Suicide Prevention programs.

In the midst of grim statistics, intense media attention, and broad government efforts, religious communities simply have not responded with the kind of biblical interpretation, theological reflection, ethical guidance, and pastoral care that their constituents need.

Basic to all other areas of ministry is the need for clarity on the biblical evidence, something that biblical scholars have been remiss in providing. My hope is that laity, clergy, and communities of faith may, with the aid of this resource, make a more informed and compassionate response to the tragic dimensions of suicide.

The present work has two basic purposes aimed at meeting some of these needs: to discuss the biblical references related to suicide and to encourage a direct response from religious communities. The biblical material is divided into direct and indirect accounts. This provides a convenient way of seeing how that material has been used to formulate or support opinions on the subject by both theologians and lay Christians. Further, the listing of texts by types of arguments shows in a unique way the influence of much "worldly wisdom" on biblical interpretation on both sides of the question.

The chapter on the history of interpretation summarizes the work of several scholars. "What does the Bible say?" on a topic is hardly worth the effort unless we also ask, "How do we *interpret* what the Bible says?" By examining the way in which the biblical texts were actually used, chapter 4 helps us to see several ways in which this important subject has been treated in the history of the church. It also makes a modest contribution to the history of exegesis.

Chapter 5 provides an overview of ethical problems related to suicide. Knowledge of the profound individual, family, and societal dilemmas posed by suicide lessens the danger that anyone will rest content with easy answers. In spite of the problems that abound, we are still called upon to confront the issue.

Following the analysis of interrelated problems, I offer a brief personal perspective on the ethics of suicide, coming to it out of a biblical/theological context. The chapter ends with a summary of what three official statements have said, followed by specific ways in which religious communities might begin their response to the current crisis. By following these guidelines, I believe individuals and groups can undertake their theological and practical tasks regarding suicide in a more responsible manner.

Several students made important contributions to my research and insight as they took directed studies on various parts of the Bible: Bonnie Farkasfalvy, Kay Hollis, Susan Lindsay, William R. Page, Thomas L. Price, and Laura Lee Wilson. Each went on to serve in local churches. It is a pleasure also to acknowledge the strong support of four other friends. Dr. Haviland Houston, former Executive Secretary of the United Methodist General Board of Church and Society, and Dean Marjorie Suchocki of Wesley Theological Seminary have been a source of encouragement at several stages of the project

Dr. Beverly Roberson Jackson, former Director of the Department of Human Welfare of the United Methodist Board of Church and Society, provided excellent leadership for the United Methodist Working Conference on Suicide. The manuscript was carefully prepared by Ms. Lucinda Brown, a former student at Wesley Seminary and now a doctoral student in New Testament at The School of Theology at Claremont.

Stefanie Ormsby Cox was as patient as she was highly efficient in seeing the book through its final stages of production, as were J. Michael West and the late John A. Hollar in the earlier phases. As an editorial team, they provided expert assistance and a rewarding sense of collegiality.

James T. Clemons

Introduction

SUICIDE IN AMERICA TODAY: STATISTICS AND DIMENSIONS

The grim statistics on suicide in America today correct many of the impressions conveyed by the communications media. If we look briefly at these statistics and what they mean, their significance and implications for American society will emerge.

A place to begin is with this appalling statistic: in 1970 the suicide rate for all age groups was 8.9 per 100,000. This figure rose to 12.6 per 100,000 in 1985.

The age group in which the percentage of suicides has remained the highest is among the elderly. Between 1970 and 1982 the suicide rate among people sixty-five and over rose 17 percent, from 15.2 to 17.8 per 100,000.[1]

Dr. Robert Butler, former director of the National Institute for the Aging and author of the Pulitzer Prize-winning book, *Why Survive? Growing Old in America*, has observed that up to twenty-five percent of all suicides occur among those over sixty-five. The highest rate is among white males in their eighties.[2]

As the overall population of the United States continues to get older, there is the danger that the number of suicides among this age group will go even higher. An article by Tad Szulc in *Parade Magazine* gave these statistics:

- Today, there are nearly 7 million Americans over age 80—the second fastest growing population group.
- By the year 2030, one-fifth of all Americans will be over 65—a leap from 30 million today to 65 million within a generation.
- The Census Bureau warned in a recent study that the rapidly expanding numbers of older people will represent a social phenomenon without historical precedent, one with serious economic implications for individuals, families, and public policymakers.[3]

Because these two sociological factors—an aging population and a high suicide rate among the elderly—are so closely related, religious communities as well as society as a whole must address both in formulating a fully informed response to the needs of the elderly. Dr. Dan G. Blazer, a psychiatrist at Duke University, predicts that if present trends continue, the number of suicides among those aged seventy to seventy-nine will eventually more than double.[4]

In spite of these statistics, most media attention has focused on age groups with the largest *number* of suicides and attempted suicides—teenagers and young adults. Current estimates are that 5,000–6,000 teenagers will die by choice this year (almost 14 per day) and perhaps thirty times that many will make the attempt.[5] But the situation is even worse than the figures indicate. The most important cause of death among young people is automobile accidents, and there is no way of knowing how many of those deaths are a form of deliberate self-destruction.

One reason for the unreliability of information on suicides is the lack of uniform practice among coroners in reporting deaths. The widespread stigma that falls on family and friends often prompts suicides to be listed as having died from other causes.

Another significant statistic, based on 1983 figures published by the United States Public Health Service, shows that it was not the fifteen to twenty-four age group that had the largest number of recorded self-inflicted deaths, but those twenty-five to thirty-four. Even among fifteen to twenty-four-year-olds, the suicide rate among those over nineteen is twice as high as those in their teens. According to the latest official figures from the National Center for Health

Statistics, in 1987 there were 4,924 deaths among those fifteen to twenty-five to thirty-four.[6] This raises the question of whether or not a particular set of social factors might have affected people in one generation in such a way that the residual suicidal tendencies have been carried over and become overt in the next age bracket. If, for example, the Vietnam conflict has had a lingering emotional effect, then it becomes important, in terms of prevention, to be attentive to the needs of those who participated in that conflict fifteen or even twenty years ago.

A somewhat bitter controversy has arisen over the impact of Vietnam on suicide among veterans. According to a United Press International Report, Dr. Norman Hearst of the University of California found that the rate of suicide among men drafted during that period was 86 percent higher than those who did not serve in that conflict.[7] Based on figures from the military draft lottery, Hearst and three of his colleagues also found that those in the first group had a death-by-motor-vehicle rate 56 percent higher than other men.

James Webb, then Assistant Secretary of Defense for Reserve Affairs, critiqued Hearst's report and the media's handling of it in an article titled "Viet Vets Didn't Kill Babies and They Aren't Suicidal."[8]

Although suicides among military personnel have been the subject of several studies and prevention programs,[9] statistics for this group are not regularly reported in the popular media. One exception, however, was a Pentagon report on the number of those who died while on active duty in 1988.[10] The number of military deaths that year was the lowest in a decade, with declines in all major categories except suicides, which rose from 247 in fiscal 1987 to 257 in 1988.

The phenomenon of "disguised" suicide is not limited to teenagers. At times it is impossible to determine when a member of the military is being truly heroic in combat and when suicidal. Our military chaplains are often at the forefront of those concerned about suicide issues, devoting themselves to prevention, and to counseling for military personnel and their families.

Children represent a very special concern. Many are murdered just before their parents commit suicide, presumably in an effort to protect them from the shame most likely to follow. But a more serious phenomenon has come to light. Psychologists now speak of "early-onset depression," a condition that often precedes and prompts suicidal behavior. This syndrome has been identified in children as early as age three. Several studies have been made on suicide among those aged ten and under.

Differences between women and men are demonstrated in a variety of social phenomena. Suicide is another area in which these differences become apparent. Whether it is the victimization that women frequently experience in work, home, or church settings, one cannot help but be alarmed when we observe that three times as many women attempt suicide as men.

On the other hand, three times as many men actually commit suicide as women. One explanation for this might be that women tend to choose a less violent form of suicide than men, such as drugs rather than guns, and thus stand a better chance of recovery. Some see this in the context of women's more frequent training in "not making a mess" or their being generally more concerned for those who will find their bodies. Although the final reasons for the difference still elude us, it certainly cannot be attributed to the myth that women are not really serious in their intent.

One rather new phenomenon in American society has been the rapid rise of suicide among blacks. Once almost unknown among that ethnic group, suicide has increased noticeably among blacks of both sexes, although more often among males. The rate doubled between 1946 and 1980.[11] News accounts often underscore the deaths of prominent, well-to-do career people as well as students and those in low-income groups who overdose on drugs, demonstrating that the phenomenon cuts across social and economic levels.

From time to time the news media go to great lengths to cover the latest outbreak of suicide among Native Americans, like that which occurred at the Wind River Reservation in Wyoming in 1986. Contrary to the impression left by reports at that time, the number of suicides among this ethnic group has remained at a very low level, according to Dr. William Hunter, Director of Mental Health Programs, Indian Health Services. He pointed out that while suicide is always a serious problem, the press seems to "discover" the situation every five years or so. "In a small area, even two can be an epidemic," he said.

But the situation may be more widespread than these comments would indicate, according to an article in *The Christian Century*. A longstanding land dispute between Navajo and Hopi tribes was legally resolved by the government when 9,000 Navajo were forced to leave their traditional homeland. The article stated that "the move has brought an increase in the suicide and disease rates among the 6,000 already taken to reservation border towns."[12]

Occasionally, members of ethnic minorities in this country hold to attitudes and values brought with them from their original cultures. One example is Fumiko Kimura, a Japanese mother despondent over the fact that her husband had been unfaithful to her. One morning early in 1985 she took her two small children and walked out into the Pacific Ocean. The children drowned, but Kimura was rescued by two college students. Although arrested and tried for murder, pleading no contest to the charge, she was reported by *The Los Angeles Times* to have received "considerable support and sympathy within the local Japanese community."[13] At her trial she was found guilty but was placed on probation.

Most Americans have long known of the accepted, and at times even honorable, place suicide holds in Japan and may think that it is the country with the highest suicide rate in the world. But it is Hungary, with a predominantly Roman Catholic population that has a self-inflicted death rate of 43.5 per 100,000, that has the highest suicide rate. The country with the second highest rate, one-third less than Hungary's, is Denmark.[14]

Another overlooked group among whom suicide has become increasingly frequent are those in prisons and jails. In a front page article of *The Washington Post* the former director of jail operations for the National Sheriff's Association, Dick Ford, called the number of such deaths "a national disgrace."[15] Lindsay M. Hayes, author of a major study on the subject, was quoted in the same article as saying, "The federal government is trying to map out a prevention strategy, but the magnitude of the problem is enormous. Even the threat of jail for a first-time offender is enough to put some people over the edge."

The problem becomes even more complex and significant when we consider the recent enactment of laws mandating incarceration for drunk drivers. These laws will result in many more "first-timers," the very group of inmates among whom the suicide rate is the highest. Both prison officials and chaplains have a special task in preventing suicide among the incarcerated.

One reason for recent attention to suicide in this segment of the population has been the increased recognition of prisoners' rights to proper care. Families of two inmates who were murdered while in jail in the District of Columbia were awarded one million dollars each for neglect in providing proper care for them,[16] and a 1986 jail suicide in Ohio resulted in a ten million dollar lawsuit against the city in which it occurred.[17] A major training resource now available on video-cassette is entitled "Suicide: The Silent Signals," produced with the help of the National Sheriff's Association and the Sheriff's Office of Suffolk County, New York.[18]

As the farm crisis continues to take its economic and emotional toll, hundreds of families each year experience depression, hopelessness, and a sense of failure, especially when they are evicted from their homes and deprived of their preferred way of life. These situations often set the stage for suicide in yet another segment of society. Although to date there has been little statistical evidence gathered on suicides among farm families, a number of articles and documentaries describe the ominous conditions.

With respect to economic levels and vocations, suicides occur more often among the affluent than among those in desperate financial circumstances. Physicians have one of the highest suicide rates, which accounts for as many as 3 percent of the deaths in their profession.[19]

Finally, we should be aware of the relationship between those who are ill and who commit suicide. A decade or so ago the suicide rate among alcoholics was fifty percent higher than for the population as a whole. This figure has now dropped to about thirty percent as a result of the increase of suicide in the general population.[20]

According to one prominent medical ethicist, the suicide rate among dialysis patients is more than one hundred times that of the general population.[21] The deaf are more prone to depression, alcoholism and suicide than are the blind. Other high-risk groups are the disenfranchised, runaways, and teenage women who have had abortions.

Suicidal behavior among homosexuals is not uncommon and is a major concern of an organization called the Federation of Parents and Friends of Lesbians and Gays.[22] Their concern is grounded in a two-edged reality: youth are in a very high risk category, and gay youth are two or three times more likely to attempt suicide than other young people.[23] This points up another area where statistics reveal an area of concern that needs a compassionate response.

Persons known to have AIDS may also be a group at high-risk of suicide. But because of the stigma attached to the disease, any reports of actual numbers or rates would probably be far from accurate. So long as stigmas exist, accurate statistics will continue to be difficult to attain, thus hindering professional efforts in the prevention of AIDS, suicide, and other life-threatening diseases and behavior.

One of the earliest signs of change in societal attitudes is found in the visual and theatrical arts. These changes have begun in relation to right-to-die issues. Millions have read or seen the play, "Whose Life Is it, Anyway?" in which a young paraplegic wins his legal right to "die with dignity" by refusing to accept forced feeding and dialysis. The television movie "Right to Die" raised similar questions. Other programs have focused on the problems of those who survive.

The real life drama has been played out in the case of quadriplegic Elizabeth Bouvia. In 1986 an appellate court in California overturned an earlier ruling and upheld Bouvia's right to starve herself rather than endure forced feeding through a nasogastric tube. That life or death decision, the court ruled unanimously, was hers alone. Bouvia has insisted that once the proper caring environment is found, she will commit suicide by refusing all food.

The moral and legal morass related to forced feeding continues. *The New York Times* reported that the American Medical Association Judicial Council had recently approved withholding all medical treatment, including food and water, from patients in irreversible comas, even when death does not appear imminent.[24] Others fear that this trend could lead to widespread and irresponsible euthanasia. Bishops of the Roman Catholic Church in the United States distributed thousands of copies of a document warning against this evil, identifying movies and television documentaries as a major danger.[25]

BEYOND THE STATISTICS: CHANGING ATTITUDES

As these statistics demonstrate, few phenomena over the past decade have had such a far-reaching impact on our society. The increased attention to suicide has come primarily because of rising rates among specific groups. The figures also indicate the geographical, ethnical, social, and financial extent of the crisis.

Even so, statistics reveal only the most obvious part of the problem. Multiply the figures by the number of bereaved family members and friends, the number of health care, social work, and prison personnel, the number of lawyers, judges, and police, and the number of rabbis, priests, pastors, and chaplains inevitably involved; then the broader dimensions of suicide become clear. A single report of a military suicide may run forty to fifty pages in length and involve numerous interviews and hearings at several locations around the country. This reality forces both society and religious communities to rethink their inherited attitudes in order to make the best possible response.

In spite of the urgent need and the high publicity that has been given the issue, churches have been conspicuously silent. Few religious groups have prepared a position paper, a reluctance underscored by the fact that one seldom, if ever, hears a sermon preached on suicide. To be sure, funeral sermons for suicides are sometimes preached, but these are necessarily restricted in scope. Their major purpose is to bring comfort and guidance to the bereaved and does not allow for the full homiletical exploration of the subject. Without the traditional benefit of solid preaching, lay people are at a severe disadvantage in addressing the issue.[26]

This may be one reason why television stories and documentaries on suicide normally portray the church, if at all, merely as presiding innocuously over the essentials in religious and social funeral rites.

The primary reason for the church's reluctance to speak out is its unexamined heritage. For centuries it has taught that suicide in any form is one of the worst of sins. At times, "self-murder" was considered equal to "blaspheming the Holy Spirit" because the one who died by his or her own hand thereby automatically forfeited any opportunity for forgiveness from the church.

Today, however, attitudinal changes are unquestionably taking place within both religious communities and society. It is important to note the ways in which these changes are manifesting themselves.

People Weekly reported the results of a lengthy reader poll to determine what Americans consider today's major sins. Suicide rated thirteenth.[27] In a Protestant adult education class at an affluent

Washington suburban church, participants were given the same poll; suicide was ranked nineteenth.

Another change is the decriminalization of both suicide and attempted suicide by most states. Laws against assisted suicides are no longer enforced as vigorously as they once were. Roman Catholic canon law was changed in 1983 to permit known suicides to receive, in some cases, full funeral rites. Since the 1960s, many insurance companies have been paying policy holders who die by suicide, provided the policy has been in effect for a year or so.

These widespread changes in society make the church's reluctance to confront the issue even more pronounced and problematic. Its failure to do so contributes to the appearance of irrelevance in today's world and of lack of concern for society's well-being. Changes in the church may begin when it starts to ask what lies behind these signs of attitudinal change in society.

Part of the answer must lie in sheer numbers. As more and more life-long Christians choose suicide, we hear less and less about their being sinners condemned to "hell" for having committed "the unpardonable sin." The social sciences, psychology and sociology, tend to absolve many suicides, saying the victim had not made a "rational" decision and instead place much of the blame for self-chosen deaths on society. And from the broader perspective of genuine altruism, if we give medals to military personnel who sacrifice themselves for others, why must we condemn civilians who take their lives in the firm belief that it will make things better for their family and friends?

A final factor in understanding why attitudes are changing is that we have once again moved into an age less likely to accept unquestioningly the authority of institutions. During the last two decades, at least since the height of the Vietnam conflict, the practices and the power of the church and the government have been radically challenged. Not only institutions but long-entrenched teachings and customs have been called into question. Others have been eradicated. Once a society almost blind to the evils of ageism, racism, and sexism, and to oppressive attitudes toward the physically and mentally marginalized, we have reached a new level of consciousness, with the result that a number of significant changes have come about. It is safe to conclude, then, that changing attitudes toward suicide are but part of the larger movement in which many old notions are being challenged.

So it is not surprising that many feel the need for a new look at the biblical material about suicide and at the way this has been interpreted through the centuries. Meeting this need to become better informed biblically can create a more humane and caring concern for those whose lives are touched by it and will provide a more secure basis on which the church and other religious communities can make an ethical response.

A WORKING DEFINITION OF SUICIDE

Before examining the biblical evidence in detail (chapters 2, 3, and 4), careful attention must be given to the matter of a proper definition of suicide. On the surface, this may seem unnecessary. Doesn't everyone know that suicide means taking one's own life? But anyone who begins to examine the matter in depth and who discusses it with others, soon realizes that such a simple definition needs qualification. For example, does one's motive determine what is labeled suicide? Does death by another's hand, when asked or commanded, fall within the definition? Do we include what have been called "shaded suicides," like deaths caused by overeating, smoking, and other forms of high-risk living, including anorexia nervosa or the "daredevil syndrome"?

The problem of definition is not as simple or irrelevant as it may seem. Psychologists, sociologists, and other professionals in the field have been wrestling with the problem of definition for years. (The first major attempt was made by the father of sociology, Émile Durkheim, in 1897, though few sociologists today would accept all that he said on the subject.)[28] Furthermore, a proper definition of suicide determines how the biblical evidence, especially in the direct accounts, is to be identified and interpreted.

Edwin Shneidman, author of *Definitions of Suicide*, reviews recent theories on definitions of suicide and other aspects of the problem, such as individual words used to refer to the act, the commonality of stimuli, stresses, purposes, goals, emotions, and internal attitudes. Shneidman then lists the implications of definition for the task of prevention. The significance of this task is set forth in his preface:

> The driving idea behind this book is the common-sense belief that effective remediation depends on an accurate assessment which, in turn, depends on meaningful definition. Prevention rests on assessment;

assessment rests on definition. When understandings are inadequate it is unlikely that effective remediations can be found. Curiously, in relation to the age-old topic of suicide, today's first order of business may well be definition.[29]

With extreme caution, he notes that the lines of thought leading to adequate definition are of various lengths:

> ...some (like religion) reach back millennia, others (like sociology) go back merely to the past century, and a few (like our supra-national concerns over nuclear destruction) begin only with our generation.[30]

Although Shneidman takes time to explain each word or phrase, his definition is worth stating.

> Currently in the Western world, suicide is a conscious act of self-induced annihilation, best understood as a multidimensional malaise in a needful individual who defines an issue for which the suicide is perceived as the best solution.[31]

This definition will not suffice for the purposes of this book or for most pastors and other students of the Bible. Some of Shneidman's explanatory comments, however, are quite helpful and will be referred to later. Other definitions, less technical and psychological in nature and coming from a more intentional religious and pastoral perspective, must now be considered.

Two definitions worth special attention appeared in the Roman Catholic publication *Suicide and the Right to Die* which included eleven articles on a wide range of topics, from recent changes in canon law to a list of more than thirty organizations in nineteen countries that now offer assistance to people who wish to choose when, where, and how they die.[32]

Niceto Blázquez, OP, Director of the Pontifical Institute of Philosophy in Madrid, began his article, "The Church's Traditional Moral Teaching on Suicide," with the statement "Suicide is the act by which a person directly, knowingly and freely brings about his or her own death." He noted that moral theologians do not include in this definition those who take their lives in a state of mental abnormality or who cannot be held responsible for their action.[33] If Blázquez's definition were held by everyone, it would obviously alter the statistics considerably, even though from a "moral" perspective, few would disagree with that position. Shneidman might even claim that by so limiting the definition, one might hinder prevention!

Somewhat along the same lines is the definition offered by Harry Kuitert, Professor of Ethics and Systematic Theology of the Free University of Amsterdam. In his article, "Have Christians the Right to Kill Themselves? From Murder to Self-Killing," he said:

> The simplest definition of suicide is the deliberate ending of one's own life, whatever the circumstances, intentions or means to achieve this end may play in the process. . . . This definition does not contain any value-judgment, but value-judgments obviously have no place in definitions.[34]

For the purposes of examining the biblical evidence, one of the components of Shneidman's definition will be used.

> *Self-Inflicted.* The fulcrum word in the definition of suicide is the word self-inflicted. If suicide is anything, it is a *mort ius dese*, a death by oneself. This would seem to be clear enough although there are problems with the biblical incident in which Saul asked another soldier to kill him and in cases of what is now called assisted suicides. But in these instances the suicidal person changes only the voice of the grammar of the event and instead of killing himself directly has himself killed at one remove only by the asked for action of another agent.[35]

Then, by use of a non-biblical example from history, Shneidman provides further clarification of the term "self-inflicted" which has further implications for our consideration.

> In the same sense the suicide is also self-inflicted even in the instance when Seneca was ordered by the mad Roman emperor Nero to kill himself. We can reasonably assume that until the moment of that imperial order, Seneca had no intention of killing himself but after the order he then consciously intended to kill himself when he did because the alternative—disgrace, enforced death, or punishment to his family—was worse.[36]

As indicated above, there are several important facets related to the task of defining suicide: (1) this task is absolutely necessary for any serious discussion of the subject; (2) those who approach the subject from different perspectives tend to formulate a definition that best facilitates their own purposes; (3) not even leading professionals within the same field can reach a consensus, or, at least, they stress different aspects of the one definition they do accept; (4) there is a wide range of "circumstances, intentions or means," each of which must conform to the basic definition.

With these considerations in mind, I offer the definition which follows for the purpose of a thorough investigation of all the biblical evidence.

Suicide is the choice and the successful completion of the act to end one's life regardless of motive, circumstance, or method.

Attention will be given in the next chapter to two attempted suicides, sometimes called parasuicides. Those acts are defined as self-initiated attempts which did not succeed as intended.

This definition is quite broad. It provides the capacity to examine the maximum range of biblical texts, particularly those in which death is self-chosen. By proceeding along this path, the understanding needed in order to be biblically informed when making a response to the current crisis is gained.

1

Suicide and Attempted Suicide in the Bible and Related Literature

In keeping with the broad definition given in the introduction, Hebrew Scriptures provide six accounts of direct suicide and the New Testament provides one. There is also one account of attempted suicide in each of the two collections. Each of these biblical texts will be examined together with references to accounts which occur at other points in biblical literature. Tracing the relationship of one text to later treatments of the same text is basic to the current form of biblical study known as canonical criticism.

What follows is not an in-depth analysis that a canonical critic would provide. It is a limited effort to see how texts related to suicide were understood at later times and under different circumstances. As such, it illustrates the fundamental fact that the history of biblical interpretation begins in the Bible itself. For example, even the two accounts of the Ten Commandments in Exodus and Deuteronomy are different in very significant ways. By comparing those two lists, one gains helpful insights into the changes in attitude and behavior that took place within the community as outward circumstances changed.

To examine and interpret texts carefully includes consideration of how the suicide or parasuicide was recorded, as well as questions such as: What did the inclusion of the story mean, or not mean, in the light of the author's original purpose in telling it? How does it fit in with the overall argument of the book in which it occurs? What attitudes toward suicide did such accounts reflect within the community? To what extent did the account help to shape later opinions?

Following a review of the biblical accounts of suicide and attempted suicide, other examples of direct accounts from 1 and 2 Maccabees, the Jewish historian Josephus, and early Christian literature will illustrate attitudes toward suicide at other points in history.

HEBREW SCRIPTURES

From the pages of the Hebrew Scriptures come familiar stories, yet they are surprising when read as accounts of either suicide or attempted suicide.

Saul and His Armor-bearer (1 Sam. 1-13; 2 Sam. 1:1-16)

The most prominent Old Testament figure recorded to have committed suicide is Saul. His long and illustrious life came to its miserable end in a battle in which three of his sons were killed, all his men were lost, and he was badly wounded. He faced the certainty of capture, ridicule, and torture by his enemies.

In a few short verses the author of 1 Samuel records the story of Saul's death in these poignant words:

> Then Saul said to his armor-bearer, "Draw your sword, and thrust me through with it, lest these uncircumcised come and thrust me through, and make sport of me." But the armor-bearer would not; for he feared greatly. Therefore Saul took his sword, and fell upon it. And when his armor-bearer saw that Saul was dead, he also fell upon his sword, and died with him. Thus Saul died, and his three sons, and his armor-bearer, and all his men, on the same day together (1 Sam. 31:4-6).

But the story continues:

> On the morrow, when the Philistines came to strip the slain, they found Saul and his three sons fallen on Mount Gilbo'a. And they cut off his head, and stripped off his armor, and sent messengers throughout the land of the Philistines, to carry the good news to their idols and to the people. They put his armor in the temple of Ash'taroth; and they fastened his body to the wall of Beth-shan. But when the

inhabitants of Ja'besh-gil'ead heard what the Philistines had done to Saul, all the valiant men arose, and went all night, and took the body of Saul and the bodies of his sons from the wall of Beth-shan; and they came to Ja'besh and burnt them there. And they took their bones and buried them under the tamarisk tree in Ja'besh, and fasted for seven days (1 Sam. 31:8-13).

As we can see, the story closes not just with Saul's tragic death, but with the account of the valiant men of Ja'besh-gil'ead, who at risk of their own lives went to retrieve Saul's body so that they might treat it with reverence and respect. Having done so, they grieved over the loss of their king.

In terms of the attitudes of the community for whom this story becomes Holy Scripture, there is no suggestion that Saul, or even his armor-bearer, were in any way to be condemned for their actions. After the death of his armor-bearer, there is no later reference to the young man, which suggests that the manner of his death was taken simply as a normal reaction under the circumstances described. From the times of the Egyptian pharaohs, perhaps earlier, servants of kings have been known to join their masters in death, either by choice or command. In other cultures, wives have also been treated in this way. With regard to the armor-bearer's motives, the young man could have feared ridicule and torture, the same as Saul. Possibly present was the fear of revealing military secrets, although at the end of a battle in which the enemy king has been killed, this possibility was quite unlikely. Finally, his suicide may have come as a result of overwhelming grief or a sense of shame for not having obeyed his king's last command. No solid clue is given regarding motive. Clearly, however, the Bible offers no condemnation of the armor-bearer's self-chosen death.

Several later passages indicate how Saul was remembered by the Israelites. Immediately after this brief, but rather detailed account of Saul's suicide, there is a different account of his death given to David by the young Amalekite (2 Sam. 1:1-16) who claims that he himself killed Saul at the king's own request. Upon hearing that blatant confession, David had the Amalekite killed, because he had dared to "put forth his hand to destroy the Lord's anointed." Of interest is the Jerusalem Bible's translation of the words attributed to Saul by the Amalekite: "Stand over me and kill me, for a giddiness has come on me, though my life is wholly in me still." "Giddiness" (shābāts, a word that occurs only here in the Hebrew Bible) here is quite ambiguous, for it can mean light-headed, insane, or even possessed of God! Today's English Version says simply, "I have been badly wounded, and I'm about to die." The New Jerusalem Bible translates Saul's statement, "Draw your sword and run me through with it; I do not want these uncircumcised men to come and make fun of me."

The prevailing but not unanimous opinion among scholars is that this later account was merely the fabrication of an ambitious young man seeking to feather his own nest by reporting a self-aggrandizing story that was not true. If one were to give credence to this second account of Saul's death, one could conceivably save Saul from any stigma which his suicide might have caused, but this would be illogical for two reasons. First, there is no indication that any such stigma was attached to his death by biblical writers. It would also leave unexplained the concise, well-stated episode that concludes 1 Samuel. The dominant view among current scholars seems the most reasonable.

As if to underscore the continuing grief of the community over Saul's death, the first chapter of 2 Samuel contains a psalm of lament:

> Ye daughters of Israel, weep over Saul,
> who clothed you daintily in scarlet,
> who put ornaments of gold upon your apparel.
> How are the mighty fallen
> in the midst of battle! (2 Sam. 1:24-25a)

Some scholars believe this psalm may have been written by David himself. In any event, he did command that it should be taught to all the people of Judah. Clearly, then, the emphasis is on the grief of David over the death of Saul, a grief apparently shared by the whole of his people. This sense of loss and grief is the basic concern of the community at the time the account was written and accepted, with no signs of concern for the manner in which the king had died.

Later, when David heard that the valiant men of Ja'besh-gil'ead had buried and honored Saul, he asked for the Lord's blessing upon them for their loyalty to their former king. That is to say, those who had honored and revered Saul, who had died by his own hand, were in turn respected and favored by David (2 Sam. 2:4b-7). By recording the story in this way, the biblical writer further shaped the idea in the minds of the Israelites that no condemnation was to be heaped upon those who treated suicides with respect.

Another account of Saul's death comes in the later tradition recorded in 1 and 2 Chronicles. Characteristic of this account is the clear elevation of David above Saul. It is not surprising, then, that the author of Chronicles would have used every opportunity to put Saul in an unfavorable light. The actual account of Saul's death by his own hand in 1 Chronicles 10 is almost identical to that given at the end of 1 Samuel. What follows, however, is not David's psalm of lament over Saul, to be sung by the people, but quite the opposite, a rather scathing epitaph to Saul's whole life:

> So Saul died for his unfaithfulness; he was unfaithful to the Lord in that he did not keep the command of the Lord, and also consulted a medium, seeking guidance, and did not seek guidance from the Lord. Therefore the Lord slew him, and turned the kingdom over to David (1 Chron. 10:13).

Of particular interest here is that, in the midst of these harsh condemnations of Saul, the chronicler, whose work is perhaps three to four centuries later than that of the accounts in 1 and 2 Samuel, did not use the manner of Saul's death against him. If there had been the slightest notion that Saul had done evil by deliberately falling on his sword, the chronicler would surely have used that incident to further his intent to put down Saul and elevate David. Our conclusion must be that even at this much later date, suicide per se was not condemned by the biblical writers or by the community for whom their writings were to become sacred scripture.

To complete the story of Saul, one more brief reference is to be noted, for he was not yet ready to rest in peace. In 2 Samuel 21, as part of a rather bizarre story involving the executions of seven of Saul's descendants, David removed the bones of Saul's body from Ja'besh-gil'ead and placed them in the tomb of his father. Thus did he offer one final tribute to the revered king. To be sure, this act can be seen as another example of David's astute political practicality. But once again there is no concern for the manner of Saul's death being used to demean his sacred memory.

In addition to this detailed attention to Saul and his armor-bearer, there are four other direct accounts of suicide in Hebrew Scriptures, each reflecting a different motive and circumstance. These we may review briefly.

Ahith'ophel (2 Sam. 17:23)

> When Ahith'ophel saw that his counsel was not followed, he saddled his ass, and went off home to his own city. And he set his house in order, and hanged himself; and he died, and was buried in the tomb of his father.

After his counsel to the would-be king Absalom had been rejected, Ahith'ophel "set his house in order" before hanging himself, thus the origin of a household phrase. The brief account ends with the simple statement which shows that he was buried without stigma or other penalty.

This biblical account is a prototype of a form of suicide that has been repeated in many cultures since, the self-death of a trusted advisor when his or her best effort has been rejected.

Zimri (1 Kgs. 16:18-19)

> And when Zimri saw that the city was taken, he went into the citadel of the king's house, and burned the king's house over him with fire, and died, because of his sins which he had committed, doing evil in the sight of the Lord, walking in the way of Jeroboam, and for his sin which he committed, making Israel to sin.

Zimri, another would-be king, had only a few days of glory before ending his own life by setting fire to his house within the city that was under siege. Although Zimri reportedly died for his sins, the manner of his death was not held against him.

History has many examples of suicide by defeated leaders, though seldom by this gruesome means. Self-chosen death under such circumstances was expected in some cultures, such as Roman society.

Samson (Judg. 16:28-31)

> Then Samson called to the Lord and said, "O Lord God, remember me, I pray thee, and strengthen me, I pray thee, only this once, O God, that I may be avenged upon the Philistines for one of my two eyes." And Samson grasped the two middle pillars upon which the house rested, and he leaned his weight upon them, his right hand upon the one and his left hand upon the other. And Samson said, "Let me die with the Philistines." Then he bowed with all his might; and the house fell upon the lords and upon all the people that were in it. So

the dead whom he slew at his death were more than those whom he had slain during his life. Then his brothers and all his family came down and took him and brought him up and buried him between Zorah and Esh'ta-ol in the tomb of Manoah his father. He had judged Israel twenty years.

After a life given largely to fighting the Philistines, Samson spent his last years blinded and tormented by his enemies. In a final act, preceded by a prayer to God for the strength to get revenge and the request that he might die with the Philistines, Samson succeeded in causing the house they were all in together to come crashing down upon them. The episode ends by crediting Samson with having killed more Philistines at his death than in all his life before. His family then came and buried him in his father's tomb. Great respect for Samson continued through the centuries and his name was included among those "heroes of faith" listed by the author of the Epistle to the Hebrews.

This account of Samson's death by choice is an example of supreme sacrifice so common among members of the world's military forces. Many Americans will recall the name of Colin P. Kelly, who flew his bomber into an enemy warship and was the first person to receive the Medal of Honor in World War II. While some would not consider such a death a suicide, it must be included within the broad definition stated above. The relationship between suicide and self-sacrifice is far more complex than it appears on the surface. Among the ethical issues raised here, and to be further considered in chapter 5, is the question of whether or not such a widely accepted form of self-sacrifice must be limited to the military.

Somewhat similar to the case of Saul are the last direct account of suicide in Hebrew Scripture, and the only attempted suicide there. In each case, death was apt to occur quite soon anyway, whether or not the requests to have someone else end their lives had been granted.

Abimelech (Judg. 9:52-54)

And Abimelech came to the tower, and fought against it, and drew near to the door of the tower to burn it with fire. And a certain woman threw an upper millstone upon Abimelech's head, and crushed his skull. Then he called hastily to the young man, his armor-bearer, and said to him, "Draw your sword and kill me, lest men say of me, 'A woman killed him.'" And his young man thrust him through, and he died.

Though exhibiting an almost laughable machismo, by our earlier definition this incident also must be considered a suicide. The account goes on to state that God thus requited Abimelech for his sins but there is nothing to suggest that the divine retribution was related to the suicide itself. If the author thought suicide was a terrible sin and was convinced that Abimelech was evil, it would have been easy to tie suicide with sin, as if to say suicide is the kind of act expected of such an evil person. In the absence of any such statement, the author implies that the manner of Abimelech's death was of no serious consequence. Further, the one clear teaching of the account, both for that time and centuries later, was that suicide was less disgraceful than being killed by a woman!

Jonah (Jon. 1–4)

The request for death by the hand of another parallels the story of Jonah. Although Jonah is not usually considered an attempted suicide, his story deserves serious consideration here. Elie Wiesel, the Nobel Prize-winning writer, details Jonah's suicidal tendencies in his book, *Five Biblical Portraits*.[1]

According to this ancient tale, Jonah was confronted by the seamen who asked, "What shall we do to you, that the sea may quiet down for us?" (Jon. 1:11). His reply reflects the psychological state of many suicidal persons today:

> Take me up and throw me into the sea; then the sea will quiet down for you; for I know it is because of me that this great tempest has come upon you (Jon. 1:12).

The crew tried first to save themselves by greater human effort to avoid Jonah's request to have them offer him as a sacrifice. At last the seamen decided they must do what Jonah had asked. For very practical reasons (the safety of the crew and boat), tinged with religious overtones (seen in their prayers for forgiveness), the men complied with Jonah's request for assistance in his own death.

The narrative does not entirely clarify Jonah's motives. The narrator may have intended to depict him as purely altruistic, wanting only to save the crew. He might have tried to portray Jonah at his wit's end in dealing with God, as other words in the passage would suggest. A final possibility is that he was mentally ill and therefore not responsible for his actions. This view is also supported by other statements made by Jonah.

When Jonah had done what he thought would result in his death, the narrative proceeds without condemning him to show how this would-be suicide not only saved the wicked city of Nineveh, but also revealed to the faithful community a significant facet of God's nature. This might suggest that God was able to use an attempted suicide as the means of accomplishing a great salvific task and revealing a profound theological truth. If ever a group of religious people who had attempted suicide were to come together for mutual support and service to others, perhaps they might choose the name "Children of Jonah."[2]

THE NEW TESTAMENT

Accounts of suicide and attempted suicide in the New Testament are rare, but the case of Judas is a familiar one.

Judas (Matt. 27:3-5; see also Acts 1:18)

> When Judas, his betrayer, saw that he was condemned, he repented and brought back the thirty pieces of silver to the chief priests and elders, saying, "I have sinned in betraying innocent blood." They said, "What is that to us? See to it yourself." And throwing down the pieces of silver in the temple, he departed; and he went and hanged himself.

This is the only direct account of suicide in the New Testament. Of the four Gospels, only Matthew makes any reference to Judas's death. This author refers to Judas as the betrayer of Jesus, but in spite of this condemnation (and contrary to some commentators) the statement that Judas hanged himself must be read simply as a statement of fact. To insist that Matthew was condemning suicide because the betrayer of Jesus died in this way is to read into the story an attitude that did not become basic Christian teaching until some three hundred years after the gospels were written.

Another account of Judas's death, however, occurs in the Book of Acts. Here there is no reference to hanging, but only to the fact that Judas fell headlong and his abdomen burst open. Again, a horrible death, but there is no indication that it was a suicide, and no explicit comment that the death came as a result of his betrayal of Jesus. It is gratuitous on the part of commentators to conflate the two accounts by explaining that Judas's fall came when the rope with which he had hung himself broke!

The Philippian Jailer (Acts 16:19-34)

The second attempted suicide in the Bible is the familiar story of the jailer at Philippi who thought he had allowed his prisoner, Paul, to escape.

> When the jailer woke and saw that the prison doors were open, he drew his sword and was about to kill himself, supposing that the prisoners had escaped. But Paul cried with a loud voice, "Do not harm yourself, for we are all here."

This account fits more easily into the category of attempted suicide than does the story of Jonah, although here the attempt was thwarted by a human and not by God through the instrument of a whale.

If we turn again to the question of motive, we may assume that the guard's thought of failure in keeping his prisoners locked up was based on the inevitable result of shame, loss of job, his own imprisonment, his possible death sentence, or all of the above. But each of these possible reasons for his suicide attempt is only speculative. The account itself does not state why he decided to take his life, only that Paul promptly and loudly intervened by honestly reporting the facts.

Again we raise the question of the author's intent in recording the story. What was his purpose in telling it in the way he did? Was it merely a necessary episode in Paul's travels? Did it show that Paul had a high regard for human life in general, and for his enemies in particular? Was he acting only out of honesty to prevent a suicide about to occur because of misinformation? Or was it part of a broad scheme to show that Paul (and, by example, other Christians) could be an effective evangelist even in the most unlikely circumstances? These questions, answered in the light of current biblical criticism, can help one decide whether or not Paul's action was based on prejudice against suicide as an inherently evil act.

This brief survey of Bible passages from several centuries of interpretation and several types of literature reveals a variety of methods, circumstances, and motives relating to the deliberate choice of persons to end their own lives. Yet this part of the biblical evidence offers no basis for the kind of outright condemnation that came in later centuries to be the church's official position. On the other hand, these texts in themselves do not provide an argument for suicide.

OTHER EARLY JEWISH LITERATURE

Suicide continued to be a well-known phenomenon in Jewish society during the Maccabean and Roman periods, which covered approximately one hundred and fifty years before the time of Jesus until the time of the first letters of Paul, some twenty years after the crucifixion. There were frequent occurrences in the church in its first three centuries. A few examples will illustrate the general attitudes of Jews and Christians toward suicide in this period.

Eleazar (1 Macc. 6:43-47)

Eleazar Avaran was a priest like his father Mattathias and a brother of Judas Maccabeus. He fought fearlessly and gave some spiritual leadership in the struggle for Jewish independence that erupted in 167 B.C.E. against the oppressive Hellenistic Syrian rule.

This famous warrior "gave himself to deliver his people and to acquire an everlasting name" by fighting to get beneath the huge elephant bearing the opposing king and slew the beast from beneath, so that it fell upon him. The brief report simply remembers the name of Eleazar Avaran as one who sacrificed himself for his nation and his cause.

Razis (2 Macc. 14:37-46)

This figure became a martyr when the oppressive ruler Nicanor sent five hundred men to Jerusalem to arrest him. Unable to resist their power, Razis made three direct attempts, one after the other, to kill himself, first by falling on his sword, then by jumping off a building, and finally by disemboweling himself and throwing his entrails at his enemies. He ended his life with a prayer that he might be restored. He has been long remembered as "Father of the Jews" because of his benevolence.

Josephus

Flavius Josephus led an illustrious life in the last third of the first century C.E. A defeated Jewish military officer in the war against Rome, he refused suicide, an option chosen by many of his comrades. He emerged from his place of siege claiming he had received a divine revelation for Vespasian, the victorious Roman general, that his captor would be the next emperor. This fortuitous circumstance enabled Josephus to enjoy a long and happy life with the Flavian family, hence his adopted name.

Recent studies by Raymond R. Newell and others of Josephus's accounts of suicide have shown that his famous historian was opposed to suicide, even though in his time "both Jews and Romans considered suicide a very honorable and, indeed, at certain times an obligatory act."[3] For the Romans, motives that could justify self-destruction included "concepts of personal honor and living in accord with nature," and, for the Jews, "concepts of God's rulership and absolute obedience to his will."[4] Both groups approved suicide as a means of avoiding an enforced way of life that was repugnant. Rabbi Eleazar specified that compassion and care should be extended to all who attempt suicide but fail.

In his *Antiquities* and *Wars*, Josephus describes Jewish mass murder/suicides to avoid Roman capture at both Gamla and Masada, but he himself believed that those who took their own lives would be punished in the afterlife. His works are still a primary source for the study of the first century of the church and were once revered for a "secular" attestation to Jesus' divinity. It is generally agreed now that this "testimony of Flavius (Josephus)" contains additions by an overly aggressive Christian scribe long after Josephus's time.[5]

EARLY CHRISTIAN LITERATURE

Voluntary martyrdom was not uncommon among the Christians of the early centuries of the church, especially in times of persecution when they faced torture or death. It was a prominent subject for theologians and biblical interpreters such as Tertullian (c. 160–224) and Origen of Alexandria (c. 185–253/254). Origen's own father committed suicide.

Among the saints who chose to have their lives end in the arena rather than recant their faith was Ignatius of Antioch, whose letters to fellow Christians in the early second century pleaded with them not to interfere with his journey to death among the animals in Rome. The extent to which one could go in seeking martyrdom is nowhere more explicit than in Ignatius's letter "To the Romans":

> I beseech you. . . . Suffer me to be eaten by the beasts that I may be found pure bread of Christ. Rather entice the wild beasts that they may become my tomb, and leave no trace of my body, that when I fall asleep I be not burdensome to any. Then shall I be truly a disciple of Jesus Christ, when the world shall not even see my body. Beseech Christ on my behalf, that I may be found a sacrifice through these instruments (4:1-2).[6]

The fourth-century church historian Eusebius (c. 260–339/40) tells of many martyrdoms in which Christians strive to be killed, at times in spite of the entreaties of their fellow believers and even enemies. One example is that of Germanicus:

> . . . who, strengthened by divine grace, overcame the natural dread of death implanted in us; although the proconsul was desirous of persuading him, and urged him from considerations of his youth, and entreated him, that he was so very young and blooming he should take compassion on himself. He, however, hesitated not, but eagerly irritated the wild beast against him, all but forcing and stimulating him, that he might the sooner be freed from this unjust and lawless generation.[7]

It was probably the frequency of suicides among Christians that prompted the venerable Saint Augustine in *City of God* to offer the first systematic argument against suicide.[8] Thus did it take more than three centuries for the church to come to the dogmatic position that suicide was a crime and a sin. Later attitudes toward suicide, including various interpretations of Scripture, will be presented in chapter 4.

SUMMARY

It should be clear, after a careful look at these direct accounts of suicide and attempted suicide, that each was told without a clear intention of condemning the act. Although in some cases the person who chose suicide was condemned by the historian, that negative

judgment was always based on how the person had lived, not how
they chose to die.

What is often overlooked is that these stories were not recorded
to make a point related to suicide. In the story of Abimelech, for
example, the writer was primarily concerned to teach that to be killed
by the hand of a woman was a shameful way to die, much worse
than asking someone else to kill you.

The next two chapters will survey a much wider range of biblical
texts that have been used to condemn or to condone suicide.

2

Does the Bible
Condemn Suicide?

Opinion regarding suicide has not been the same in every age. As attitudes have changed over the centuries, a wide variety of biblical texts have been used both to condemn and to condone the acts of suicide and attempted suicide.

Chapter 1 noted in detail specific accounts of such acts from Jewish and Christian writers in the centuries just before and after the time of Jesus. Chapter 4 will trace the development of Christian and Jewish thought on the subject from Saint Augustine to the present, focusing on interpretations of biblical texts discussed here and in chapter 3. It will not be possible to cover all the philosophical and literary treatments of suicide, although some of the ideas expressed in those non-biblical sources have often influenced the way various parts of the Bible were interpreted.

First, those texts used to condemn suicide will be reviewed. Three types of arguments, each with supporting biblical evidence, have been offered.

God is the sole creator of all life, so only God can end life. This belief puts any choice to end one's life entirely beyond human reach. If this is true, how can we justify efforts to save or prolong life without violating the same principle? The answer is based on the corollary assumption that any gift from God is good and is to be preserved

whenever possible. But further questions arise: how far are we to
go to keep someone alive, and under what circumstances may one
life be sacrificed for another? These ethical questions require further interpretation (see chapter 5).

*God, through biblical injunctions, has specifically forbidden the
taking of one's own life.* This belief is based on interpretation of biblical
texts in which suicide is not specifically mentioned. While the belief
is widely held, most careful students of the Bible agree that there
are no specific injunctions against suicide.

*God, through the Bible, has given us accounts of the lives of
those who refused to die by their own hands even in the midst of suffering. These stories are examples for us to follow.* In spite of the
fact that several suicides are recorded, other texts show clearly that
this response to life's vicissitudes, however painful they may be, is
to be rejected.

Related to this is the notion that by taking one's own life, a person
concedes to human weakness and fails his or her obligation to community (either secular or religious), family, and friends. That is, one
cannot fulfill one's purpose in life if one deserts one's post of duty.

SOME WORDS OF CAUTION

Keep some words of caution in mind in the following discussion of
the texts. First, the biblical writers were not specifically concerned
about suicide as they wrote the passages being considered. Their
works were not set out in neat, orderly categories, nor were their
authors aware of the kinds of questions later generations have wanted
the Bible to answer.

Second, to interpret texts without regard for their unsystematic and
historically limited character increases the danger of reading into a particular passage either a prohibition or a justification of suicide that
originates in our own thinking, not in the text itself. This error, eisegesis (reading into the text one's previously held views), is not unlike
the interpretation of Judas's death mentioned in chapter 1. That account,
entirely apart from what the evangelist Matthew was intending, has
often been read as a prohibition against suicide. Others have seen Judas's
act as evidence of his repentance and an effort to atone for his sin after
he had been rejected by those who had paid him.[1]

Obviously, eisegesis is not a deliberate act. Many ways that are not always recognizable will lead us to the conviction that a text does in fact support our position. The spirit or mood of the times often aids our acceptance of questionable biblical interpretation. To lessen the danger of the excesses which eisegesis so often brings, biblical scholars have often adhered to the principles of the historical-critical method, which stresses the need to find the author's original intention. That approach, while no guarantee of infallible results, has proven an effective safeguard against making a text say only what we want it to say.

The extremes to which careless biblical interpretation can go were noted by John Donne in his work, *Biathanatos*. In it, he argued—from nature, reason and God (by which he meant largely the Bible)—why suicide should not be universally condemned. Speaking of those who "think they have the light and authority of scripture" to support their opinions, Donne said:

> They take any small text of scripture that mistakenly appears to them to be of use in justifying any opinion of theirs. Then, since the word of God has that precious nature of gold so that a little quantity by reason of faithful tenacity and malleability can be made to cover 10,000 times as much as any other metal, they extend that small text so far, and labor and beat it to such a thinness that it is hardly any longer the word of God. They do so simply to give their reasons a little tincture and color of gold, even though they have lost all its weight and value.
>
> But since the scripture itself teaches that "No prophecy in the scripture is of private interpretation" (2 Pet. 1:20), the whole church is not bound and enclosed by the fancy of any one (or of a few) who, being content to put themselves to sleep with any opinion and lazy prejudice, dream up arguments to establish and authorize it.[2]

The last word of caution before turning to the texts themselves is that the division between those which condemn and those which condone suicide has been based on the arguments of theologians and other thinkers from biblical times to the present. They are not made as a result of my own study. My hope is that one result of this presentation of the evidence will be to make biblical commentators more sensitive to the matter of suicide, both at points where it deserves attention and where it is not to be inserted into the text's meaning.

TEXTS CONDEMNING SUICIDE
FOR VIOLATING GOD'S CREATION

The belief that life is a gift of God, the creator and ruler of the universe, is foundational among biblical writers and for most of those who establish their faith and theology on Scripture. Even those who condone suicide from a biblical perspective will usually agree with this belief. But others go on to say that because of this divine gift of life, God alone has the power to take it away. That power is not to be contradicted or questioned. Based on that theological affirmation of God's right, the following texts have been interpreted in a way that precludes suicide.

The Creation Stories (Gen. 1:1–2:4a, 2:4b-25)

The assertion that God is the creator of all life is emphasized by the position of these stories at the beginning of the oldest and most revered section of Hebrew Scripture. That there are in reality two separate accounts of creation in Genesis, representing separate Hebraic traditions that came to be placed one after the other, has been the opinion of most biblical scholars for well over a century. In each story, God alone is the ultimate source of life, although some would see in Genesis 1:1-2 the possibility that lifeless matter in some form preceded that divine act of bringing all forms of life into being.

From such a foundation have come a host of theological conclusions related to God's sole prerogative to create, sustain, and redeem all life that ever was, has been, and will be (see also Prov. 8 and John 1:1-14).

Blood for Blood (Gen. 9:6)

> Whoever sheds the blood of man, by man shall his blood be shed; for God made man in his own image.

In his detailed study of *Biblical Perspectives on Death*, Lloyd R. Bailey cited this verse in which God is speaking to Noah as a prime example of the way human life was valued as a result of having been created by God.

> The power of life is envisioned as belonging intrinsically to the Deity, and it is given to creatures only through a special creative act (Gen. 2:7; Ps. 104:30). . . . The taking of human life . . . is such an

arrogant usurpation of power that execution [of the offender] must result.[3]

The last statement could fall into the next category regarding specific commands against suicide, but it is cited here because of Bailey's accurate assessment of the several understandings of death in Hebrew Scriptures and of the sanctity of life in ancient Israel. Referring to this verse in that context, he added:

> Thus if life does not have such absolute value as to forbid execution, at least execution is perceived as the only fitting penalty for violating its sanctity.[4]

Attitudes toward death were often expressed in terms of bloodletting and blood atonement. This association was a characteristic of many social contracts and religious covenants (see Lev. 17).

The move from this high estimation of life to a condemnation of homicide, as well as suicide, is short and clear. At the same time, it leaves open the inevitable question of whether legal exceptions for homicide, such as war, might not allow exceptions to suicide also.

Life Belongs to God (1 Sam. 2:6)

> The Lord kills and brings to life;
> he brings down to Sheol and raises up.

Once again, we have a text that easily lends itself to being an injunction against suicide. If only the Lord "kills," it follows that no one can usurp that divine prerogative by taking one's own life. The implicit theology is that every death must be ascribed to God (see also Wisd. of Sol. 16:13).

The Lord Gave (Job 1:20-21)

> Then Job arose, and rent his robe, and shaved his head, and fell upon the ground, and worshiped. And he said, "Naked I came from my mother's womb, and naked I shall return; the Lord gave, and the Lord has taken away; blessed be the name of the Lord."

The book of Job is an example of human beings seeking a philosophical understanding of life rather than the practical side of Wisdom, the mere application of maxims (see also Prov. 8). To read it as the historical account of an unfortunate individual who chooses simply to endure "the slings and arrows of outrageous fortune" is to miss its profound wrestling with questions of theodicy, the goodness of God in the midst of human misery and natural calamity. A simplistic reading makes Job little more than a good Greek Stoic and reduces the whole emphasis to the human realm. Yet question upon theological question comes tumbling forth from the story, particularly from the conversations between Job and his friends. In spite of such theological depth, however, Job has long been taken as an example of one who, in spite of extreme human misery, refused to take his own life.

The verses cited above come from a much later date in Israel's history than those examined earlier. They show that a continuing tenet of faith was God's sovereign right both to create life and to take it away. Not only are the two ideas here inextricably linked, they are accepted with the ultimate allegiance, Blessed be the name of the One who alone both gives and takes away.

I Kill and I Make Alive (Deut. 32-39)

> See now that I, even I, am he,
> and there is no god beside me;
> I kill and I make alive;
> I wound and I heal;
> and there is none *that can* deliver
> out of my hand   [italics mine]

Thomas Aquinas cited this verse as an admonition against suicide: because only God created life, only God could reserve the right to take life. In their historical context, however, the words had a quite different intent. The verse comes from one of Moses' sermons to the Israelites before they entered the land of their enemies, assuring them that their God was stronger and would outlast the gods of the peoples into whose land they were about to enter. To use the verse as a condemnation against suicide moves well beyond this original intention.

Divine Prerogative (Ps. 104:27-30)

> These all look to thee,
> to give them their food in due season.
> When thou givest to them, they gather it up;
> when thou openest thy hand,
> they are filled with good things.

> When thou hidest thy face, they are dismayed;
> when thou takest away their breath, they die
> and return to their dust.
> When thou sendest forth thy Spirit,
> they are created;
> and thou renewest the face of the ground.

This marvelous hymn to the Creator moves to its conclusion with the theological affirmation that both the giving of life and the taking in death are divine prerogatives. This is similar to what was noted above. But again, whether applied to either suicide or homicide, the same problems exist.

Who Finds Me Finds Life (Prov. 8:34-36)

> Happy is the man who listens to me,
> watching daily at my gates,
> waiting beside my doors.
> For he who finds me finds life
> and obtains favor from the Lord;
> but he who misses me injures himself;
> all who hate me love death.

One of the superb literary texts of the Bible, Proverbs 8 is an incomparable personification of Wisdom, extolling its origins with God (v. 23), its essential relationship to justice (v. 8), and its aggressive appeal to all, not unlike that of a temptress, which is no doubt an ironic attack on the unwise behavior of the day (vv. 2-4). Wisdom holds inherent value for the one who possesses it (vv. 10-11).

The chapter reflects the philosophical dimension of the ancient Wisdom movement, over against the practical dimension of the simple adages found throughout most of the book. The thrust is not unlike that of Socrates's observation that "the unexamined life is not worth living." Yet the ascription of praise is to God for the marvelous gift of wisdom, which provides the means both of finding God and of obtaining God's favor. This is the basis for life. By implication, death is a failure to find, or a failure to accept, the divine gift of wisdom, as God intended at the beginning of his work. Those who deliberately reject wisdom love that which is contrary to the life God intended. To love death, which is implied in suicide, is to go against God.

A Time for Everything (Eccl. 3:1-3)

> For everything there is a season,
> and a time for every matter under heaven:
> a time to be born, and a time to die;
> a time to plant, and a time to pluck what is planted;
> a time to kill, and a time to heal;
> a time to break down, and a time to build up.

A few years ago an award-winning home for the elderly built a lovely chapel as part of its new facilities. It was decided that the ten stained glass windows at the back would depict themes from this chapter in Ecclesiastes. Some wondered aloud why a biblical text on the apparent meaninglessness of life should be the subject of windows in a beautiful chapel for the elderly. The answer was, who else could better understand the meaning of time and of life's timespan?

The implication of these and other verses can be seen as supporting the view that "our times," whatever they may be or however long they may be, are in God's hands, not ours. This interpretation would be consistent with the texts discussed above.

To be sure, most of the words spoken by "the Preacher" (Ecclesiastes) are indeed depressing. The book itself represents one of the common stages in the development of a wisdom movement, that of despair and meaninglessness. The ancient literature of Mesopotamia, Egypt, and Greece went through such a stage. In its worst form, it becomes totally nihilistic, as is also seen in much modern thought.

Seen in this light, the words of Ecclesiastes are at best a grudging concession to the necessity of life's mere endurance, without hope of meaning or reward. Those predisposed to suicide on other grounds can look to this work as offering some justification for the act (see chapter 3).

In Him Was Life (John 1:1-5)

> In the beginning was the Word, and the Word was with God, and the Word was God. He was in the beginning with God; all things were made through him, and without him was not anything made that was made. In him was life, and the life was the light of men. The light shines in the darkness, and the darkness has not overcome it.

Once again the theme of God's creation of life "in the beginning," coupled with God's continual provision of light and life, is set forth, this time at the beginning of a Gospel. Thus, the opening verses of John's Gospel are, in one sense, another creation story (see also Prov. 8). From at least the Middle Ages the author of the Fourth Gospel has been depicted in manuscript illumination, mosaics, icons, and stained glass windows as "John the Theologian."

As "theologian" (he was historian as well), John begins his account of what God did in Jesus Christ by reiterating God's right and power to create life. That life was to be used in a special way, namely to enlighten humanity so that it would shine on through whatever darkness men and women might encounter. While the theme of life continues throughout John's Gospel, the theme of Word (*logos* in Greek) is virtually dismissed, except that Jesus Christ is viewed at every point as "accomplishing" what God's Word was sent out to do (compare Isa. 55:11).

From this theological emphasis on Christ's coming to give life and to enable others to "have it more abundantly," the conclusion can easily be drawn that death, including death by choice, is contrary to God's intent, both in creation and in the sending of Christ to be the source of both life and light in the world. At this point, of course, the interpretation has not dealt with the meaning of life. That subject will come up in the next chapter, where some of the Johannine literature will be considered as a means of condoning suicide.

TEXTS CONDEMNING SUICIDE
AS A VIOLATION OF GOD'S COMMANDMENT

The next group of texts contains passages that have been used to argue against suicide for a different reason, namely the belief that they imply a specific prohibition against the act.

The Commandment (Exod. 20:13; Deut. 5:17)

You shall not kill.

One of the problems of adhering to this commandment has been the variant interpretations of the Hebrew word *qatal*, "to kill" or "to murder." The distinction is important to the discussion of whether or not any form of killing under any circumstance is ever justified. Most commentators agree that the intent was basically to keep individual

Israelites from taking the law into their own hands when tempted to do violence to their neighbors.

Saint Augustine drew heavily upon this commandment to condemn anyone who committed suicide. Only grudgingly did he concede that on rare occasions God might have directed past saints (those already canonized by the church) to take their own lives!

Arguments against self-killing (or self-murder) will be but extensions of those against homicide, the only difference being whether or not one has an inherent right to do with one's own life what one is forbidden to do with another's. But if one cannot treat one's self differently from the way one treats others on the basis that all "selves" are the creation of and belong to God, then suicide is at least as wrong as homicide. Apparently Saint Augustine found less reason to support self-murder than murder, the killing of another. The distinction between self-killing and self-murder can be appreciated in the same way that society as well as the church distinguish between killing and murder. Not all killings are condemned the way murder is condemned. There are also degrees of murder, some more severely punishable than others, and there are some killings that are not considered murder. To insist on self-murder is by its very nature unduly prejudicial. Yet both have been used.[5]

Keep Your Soul (Deut. 4:9)

> Only take heed, and keep your soul diligently, lest you forget the things which your eyes have seen, and lest they depart from your heart all the days of your life; make them known to your children and to your children's children.

Rabbis have long used this text, together with Genesis 9:5, and the example of Job, to argue that suicide was wrong. Keeping the soul, understood only as life on earth, was necessary in order to pass on the faith to later generations.

Choose Life (Deut. 30:19)

> I call heaven and earth to witness against you this day, that I have set before you life and death, blessing and curse; therefore choose life, that you and your descendants may live.

These words once more stress God's intent that Israel, as a people, should live. It is difficult even to imagine that individual suicide was at all in the mind of the writer. Moses is here speaking to those soon to cross the Jordan River about how they are to live once they enter into the new land. As the preceding verses (vv. 15-18) make clear, the whole people of God are to obey all the commandments, statutes, and ordinances. The result of an idolatrous life, by contrast, is not physical death to the entire community, but that death which is the state of being unfaithful.

By extension, one may conclude that life is to be lived obediently and faithfully in order that all the people, and each individual, might live to worship and serve God in the beauty and happiness of holiness.

Why Will You Die? (Ezek. 18:31-32)

Cast away from you all the transgressions which you have committed against me, and get yourselves a new heart and a new spirit! Why will you die, O house of Israel? For I have no pleasure in the death of anyone, says the Lord God; so turn, and live.

When read with the question of suicide in mind, these words seem to be God's way of excluding such an act from divine favor. Speaking through the prophet, God expresses in a negative statement a love for the life of each person. Any death, including that of a suicide, is unpleasing to God. This was another of the texts to which Augustine turned in condemning suicide, even though the context shows that it was probably intended to apply neither to individuals nor to all humanity. Instead, it is a passage addressed directly to the house of Israel, calling upon that religious *community* to be faithful to the divine commands, especially those that pertained to justice.

Also problematic, and a point arguing against a universal, unqualified love of every person, is the questionable, ungracious theological position in verses 25-29, wherein life and death are based strictly on righteousness and wickedness. Only by the use of restrictive blinders to the context of these verses can they be used to condemn the specific act of suicide.

Fear (Matt. 10:28; Luke 12:4-5)

And do not fear those who kill the body but cannot kill the soul; rather fear him who can destroy both soul and body in hell.

The opening lines indicate that fear is not to be removed entirely. Fear needs to be redirected. As such, it is a therapeutic threat, designed to make the one who fears do so for the right reason. By a rather circuitous form of reasoning, the person contemplating suicide is thus urged to fear God, and so obey the all-powerful One, rather than to fear oneself, who can kill only the body. In terms of suicide, this is a theological statement, not a psychological one.

You Are Not Your Own (Cor. 6:19-20)

> Do you not know that your body is temple of the Holy Spirit within you, which you have from God? You are not your own; you were bought with a price. So glorify God in your body.

To be called the temple of the Holy Spirit indicates that the human body is held in high esteem by God. These verses call for both proper care and proper use of our bodies. Because the body is so precious to God, indeed, the very dwelling place of God, nothing is to be done to harm it.

From this understanding of the text, it is easy to see why it could be used as an admonition against self-destruction. It has been directed particularly to those prone to follow high-risk life-styles, whether or not their behavior was intentionally suicidal. How could we presume to destroy that which is so holy, which we are not even to abuse?

The author's concern is not only for what ultimately happens to the body, in its physical nature, but also for the effect of its use or misuse on one's relationship to God. In this chapter, there is a theological as well as practical concern.

A major part of our understanding of the text rests on Paul's varying uses of the term body (Greek, *soma*). Since the work of Rudolph Bultmann in the middle third of this century, the intimate, theological dimension of body in Paul's thought has brought a reconsideration of passages where he used that term. Here, for example, Paul is not merely pronouncing another moral tenet, as he sometimes does by use of the vice lists of the day (see chapter 3). Rather, he focuses on each person's relationship to Christ's body, the church. Thus it could be argued that it was not the harm done to the physical body that Paul is arguing against, but its unfaithful use in a way that separated the whole person from God.

Initial Presumption (Eph. 5:29)

For no man ever hates his own flesh, but nourishes and cherishes it, as Christ does the church.

Although the author of these words (some scholars question Paul's authorship of this epistle) is concerned here primarily with both ecclesiology and Christian family relationships, the verse has been used to show how contrary suicide is to ordinary human experience. Paul's arguments, like those of Jesus and other biblical figures, occasionally were supported by what we might call "common sense," that is, the general, normative behavior of most people most of the time in a given culture. Even today, Christian ethics relies on what J. Philip Wogaman has termed "initial presumption."[6]

This statement is somewhat buried in a longer discussion of the church and of the way husbands should love and care for their wives. The church was always in danger of putting itself in a bad light before society whenever it failed to live up to the standards of mutual respect and dignity among its own members. For husbands not to love their wives as their own bodies was, in effect, to ridicule the body of Christ before the whole world. Clearly, the injunction relates to the matter of spouse abuse in any age, condemning that particular heinous sin on both ecclesiological and christological grounds. as well as on moral and legal ones.

The relevance of this text in condoning suicide must be seen in its "initial presumption," the kind of normal behavior one takes toward one's body and one's life. To the extent that we are disposed to care for ourselves, we would not harm, much less destroy ourselves.

That You May Stand (Eph. 6:10-13)

Finally, be strong in the Lord and in the strength of his might. Put on the whole armor of God, that you may be able to stand against the wiles of the devil. For we are not contending against flesh and blood, but against the principalities, against the powers, against the world rulers of this present darkness, against the spiritual hosts of wickedness in the heavenly places. Therefore take the whole armor of God, that you may be able to withstand in the evil day, and having done all, to stand.

No stronger metaphor of the Christian as a soldier on duty, with ongoing responsibilities, can be found in the Scriptures. The several commands—"be strong," "put on," "take," "pray," and "keep alert"—as well as the possibilities—"that you might stand" and "that you may be able to withstand"—are all in the Greek present tense. This means that the action is to continue; it is not an action done only once or an action that has been completed.

There is no hint here that the reader is to have any thought whatever of leaving her or his post in order to "be with the Lord." The passage ends (vv. 18-20) with Paul, even though in chains, seeking the prayers of his followers that he might continue to live in order to keep on proclaiming the gospel (see also 1 Cor. 16:9).

Endure Through Persecution (1 Pet. 1:6-9)

In this you rejoice, though now for a little while you may have to suffer various trials, so that the genuineness of your faith, more precious than gold which though perishable is tested by fire, may redound to praise and glory and honor at the revelation of Jesus Christ. Without having seen him you love him; though you do not now see him you believe in him and rejoice with unutterable and exalted joy. As the outcome of your faith you obtain the salvation of your souls.

The testing of faith through persecution comes with the promise and reward of salvation for those who endure. The writer of 1 Peter did not regard suicide as the antithesis of such endurance. Rather, he attacked sub-Christian behavior that must have been all too evident among his contemporary readers.

So put away all malice and all guile and insincerity and envy and all slander (1 Pet. 2:1).

Not only are Christians to be loving and at peace with one another, they are also to get along with a hostile society. This will enable them to heed the specific injunctions to "live as free men . . . live as servants of God" (1 Pet. 2:16).

The entire letter stresses the necessity of righteousness and legal living, even though the "end of all things is at hand" (1 Pet. 4:7). The poignant admonition is based on the final reality of God's peace, love and holiness, which in turn calls for selfless love to others. In short, Christians are called to express genuine faithfulness to the very end.

Hold on to Life (Rev. 2:10-11)

> Do not fear what you are about to suffer. Behold, the devil is about
> to throw some of you into prison, that you may be tested, and for
> ten days you will have tribulation. Be faithful unto death, and I will
> give you the crown of life. He who has an ear, let him hear what
> the Spirit says to the churches. He who conquers shall not be hurt
> by the second death.

Sufferings in this life sent as divine testing is an idea at least
as old as the Book of Job. It is found in the apocalyptic literature
of Daniel and Revelation. This response is acceptable to many when
questions of God's goodness arise, like Where is God in the midst
of all this evil? Why is God doing this to us? or even, What did we
do to deserve such divine punishment?

The relationship between suicide and misfortune is well-
documented throughout history, from some of the direct accounts
in the Bible to contemporary American society. Financial failures
following the stock market crash of 1929, the tragedies of Vietnam
in the sixties, and the pressures of life for youth in the eighties show
that correlations between the two are not hard to recognize or to
understand.

Human misery has long been the concern of philosophers and
theologians. Biblical writers not only noted the fact; they gave reasons
why such pain is necessary and, at times, promised reward for those
who endured it. The endurance of life's difficulties, no matter how
severe, was an expression of faithfulness.

Such a message would be aimed primarily, as in Daniel and
Revelation, toward those who might be tempted by apostasy. The
chief aim of apocalyptic literature was to convince the faithful not
to give up by renouncing their faith. It seeks to accomplish this goal
by providing a plausible explanation: God is just about to intervene
to set things right, so hold on a little longer!

This message can also be an encouragement to the faithful not
to give in by committing suicide. Withstanding such pressure was
basic to Greek and Roman philosophy, especially the Stoics. Stoicism
was a widely practiced philosophy in the world of the New Testament. It is not surprising to find its influence on Christian thought
and ethics. The text from Revelation is but one of several examples.
A certain irony is to be noted in this "stoic" attitude *against* suicide,

for the followers of Zeno (342?–270?) considered suicide favorably as the last bastion of the individual against all the evils life could bring.[7]

Although the text cited can easily be applied to the issue of suicide, the original intent was for the early Christian community to avoid apostasy: it was really the Devil who was tempting the faithful to renounce their beliefs. The specific threat of ten days in prison highlights the very short duration of the problem before divine help comes.

In the midst of any inclination toward suicide, most counselors today would agree that specific intervention is called for, especially when it is offered in the spirit of genuine loving concern and with the consent of the person involved. Impulses toward suicide, they find, are usually of limited duration, and even those who make the attempt often show strong ambivalence, desiring life as much as death.

Thus the injunction to hold on to life can have meaning in the prevention of suicide, even though the kinds of official persecution associated with the Book of Revelation are not normally present.

Before turning to a third type of text used to condemn suicide, consider one more biblical angle on the way humans are expected to endure. The creation stories have a bearing on anti-suicide interpretations. To develop this point of view, some historical background is needed. First, a church father, Augustine, spoke indirectly about suicide. Fedden noted that one of the arguments used by Augustine was a somewhat curious twist of the basic Stoic approval of suicide.

> The truly noble soul [Augustine] said, will bear all suffering; to escape, even when there is no reason for staying, is testimony of weakness.[8]

Second, earlier in history, the Emperor Hadrian had considered suicide a crime, equal to desertion, and declared that the attempt to commit suicide was punishable by death itself. From these two, the idea of enduring, not deserting, one's post is formulated and could be applied to biblical material from the creation stories.

In the passages that tell of the divine image in male and female (Gen. 1:27) and of the creation of man and woman (Gen. 2:7, 21), God also appointed them to have specific functions within the created order:

> And God blessed them, and God said to them, "Be fruitful and multiply, and fill the earth and subdue it; and have dominion over the fish

of the sea and over the birds of the air and over every living thing
that moves upon the earth" (Gen. 1:28).

The Lord God took the man and put him in the garden of Eden
to till it and keep it (2:15).

Then the Lord God said, "It is not good that the man should be
alone; I will make him a helper fit for him" (2:18).

These appointments to specific functions in the created order
could be viewed as commands to a post of duty grounded in the creation stories themselves. It could then be argued, along the lines of
Hadrian and Augustine, that these commands were for all humans.
Since they have not been rescinded, the orders are to be obeyed with
as much fidelity today as when first issued. One does not have the
right to disobey such a divine command by committing suicide.

In an age of ecological crisis and a potential nuclear holocaust,
the responsibilities implicit in the creation stories are seen in terms
of care-taking in the earth-garden, which God pronounced "very
good." The natural resources so essential to the life God gave are
not, as once fancifully imagined, either limitless or indestructible.
Thus, "Take care!" is a command with increasingly vital significance
for faithful individuals and communities.

PERSONS WHO CHOSE TO LIVE

Along the lines of Stoic endurance, but without the Stoic acceptance
of suicide, the following texts have been read by Christians as evidence
against that act. The primary assumption is that because these biblical
characters suffered without giving up or giving in, they are to be
taken as models of true faithfulness. Suicide, then, is wrong for yet
another biblical reason, even though the idea motivating this particular idea originated among non-biblical authors and was not applied to the biblical figures until long after the time of their original
characterization in the biblical texts.

God Will Provide (Ps. 23:1)

The Lord is my shepherd, I shall not want; . . . .

Like so many other Psalms, this most beloved one touches a common theme: in times of trouble, faithful people for ages untold have
turned to God to deliver them from suffering, oppression, and

impending death. The implication is that in the extremities of life, this spiritual response is always preferable to any other alternative. It is the essential first step (see also, among others, Ps. 77, 86, 88, and 139).

The Tenacity of Job (Job 2:9-10)

> Then his wife said to him, "Do you still hold fast your integrity? Curse God, and die." But he said to her, "You speak as one of the foolish women would speak. Shall we receive good at the hand of God, and shall we not receive evil?" In all this Job did not sin with his lips.

In addition to what has already been said about the character of Job, we can see how his tenacious clinging to life is a prime model of human endurance. The references to "the patience of Job" are anything but appropriate to the biblical figure who screamed his charges against God for bringing such miseries upon him, cursed the day he was born, and protested vehemently by saying that no human sin, however vile, deserved punishment such as his. Yet his refusal to heed his wife's caustic, though practical and possibly well-intentioned plea is central to the book: Job refused steadfastly to "curse God and die."

Although the final justification for Job is made with reference to his lips, we may assume that the violation in words would be the immediate cause of death at the Lord's hand. Thus, by not heeding his wife's pleas, he was in effect rejecting the notion of suicide, in spite of extreme physical privation and deep emotional suffering.

The author makes it very clear that Job did not curse God "with his lips," even though he later challenged God as severely as anyone in Scripture, including the most irate of the Psalmists. Only by extension can these verses be applied to suicide per se, but such extension, in the light of the whole book, is easily and often made.

One final comment is that this profound book merely uses the misfortunes of a man named Job as the literary setting for one of the greatest treatments of theodicy, the question of God's presence or absence in the midst of human misery.

Jonah and Other "Suicidal" Persons

The stories of Jonah, Elijah, certain of the Psalmists, and, at times, Paul, illustrate that regardless of their despondency, and their pleas to be delivered from the miseries of this life, God did not grant their request. Furthermore, they themselves did not take any of the opportunities available to them. Only Samson had such a prayer answered and that was in a unique circumstance, a plea to have one last military victory over the hated Philistines.

Martyrdom or Suicide (Matt. 4:5-7; Luke 4:9-12)

> Then the devil took him to the holy city, and set him on the pinnacle of the temple, and said to him, "If you are the Son of God, throw yourself down; for it is written, 'He will give his angels charge of you,' and 'On their hands they will bear you up, lest you strike your foot against a stone.'" Jesus said to him, "Again it is written, 'You shall not tempt the Lord your God.'"

Jesus' refusal to be tempted by the devil to throw himself off the temple (probably from a corner of the temple grounds into the valley below) is sometimes seen as a reason why Christians should not commit suicide. This interpretation of the story overlooks the literal meaning of the devil's intent, which was not to invite Jesus to commit suicide. Rather, the temptation was for Jesus to prove that he could live through the fall and thus win the glory of the world. It was to prevent this perversion of his mission that Jesus steadfastly refused to jump.

Along the same lines, Augustine argued that Jesus' refusal to throw himself down was reason enough for Christians not to commit suicide, even in the face of severe persecution, much less in the face of lesser temptations or hardships.

Fedden's comment on this is fitting:

> This whole question of martyrdom and suicide is strange, and histories of the times fill one alternatively with horror and admiration. Faith and courage have perhaps never existed in such degree among large numbers of people as among the early Christians. One can only admire these virtues. Their passionate disregard for life, however, involves other questions: there seems something a little perverted in their welcome of pain and a sort of biological insanity in their determination to destroy their flesh and root out their own lives. As Donne says, that age was so hungry and ravenous of martyrdom, "that many were baptized only because they would be burnt."[10]

God Works for Good (Rom. 8:28)

> We know that in everything God works for good with those who love
> him, who are called according to his purpose.

This oft-quoted assurance has sustained Christians across the ages
in the midst of personal doubt, perplexity, fear, anxiety, and oppression. Its value in calling the faithful to trust in God's wisdom and
love has been proven in the experiences of untold numbers. As such,
it is often used to give strength and courage, if not always enlightenment and swift answers, to one's personal pain and problems.

Obviously, the text could have value in helping a committed
Christian contemplating suicide to rely on that trust in God when
confronting a seemingly hopeless situation. It would also be of value
for those friends and family members whose lives are grieved by
a suicide. Finally, it could speak to those who, having attempted
suicide, must begin to deal with the reality that, once again, they
have been given a new gift of life, like it or not. They must now
decide how to use that gift.

Unnecessary Martyrdom (2 Cor. 11:30-32)

> If I must boast, I will boast of the things that show my weakness.
> The God and Father of the Lord Jesus, he who is blessed for ever,
> knows that I do not lie. At Damascus, the governor under King Ar'etas
> guarded the city of Damascus in order to seize me, but I was let down
> through a window in the wall, and escaped his hands.

There is a tendency among some Christians to rush into martyrdom. Here Paul offers an example of his own refusal to be captured
in order to continue his mission to evangelize the Gentiles. Though
he was no stranger to prisons (2 Cor. 11:23-28 offers the account
of his own sufferings) and was able to use even that unlikely situation as an occasion for some of his best work in personal evangelism,
church administration, and theological reflection, he nevertheless was
not one to give himself up to every opportunity to be incarcerated.

Over the past twenty years, especially since the publications of
Günter Bornkamm's *Paul* and Hans Conzelmann's *The Theology of
Saint Luke*, much scholarly attention has been given to the question
of where we are to find the best sources for understanding Paul's
life.[11] Frequently the long biographical account in the Book of Acts

seems at variance with the autobiographical fragments in the epistles. Although several issues are still debated, most scholars maintain that both sources are necessary. In this passage is a point of agreement. Paul was not among those who would opt for prison or death, either to prove his faithfulness or to escape the troubles of the world. God's grace, the theme of much of his writing, was sufficient to remove the temptation of a premature and unnecessary martyrdom.

When I Am Weak, Then I Am Strong (2 Cor. 12:7-10)

And to keep me from being too elated by the abundance of revelations, a thorn was given me in the flesh, a messenger of Satan, to harass me, to keep me from being too elated. Three times I besought the Lord about this, that it should leave me; but he said to me, "My grace is sufficient for you, for my power is made perfect in weakness." I will all the more gladly boast of my weaknesses, that the power of Christ may rest upon me. For the sake of Christ, then, I am content with weaknesses, insults, hardships, persecutions, and calamities; for when I am weak, then I am strong.

Paul may once again be taken as a model of one who, though wanting and even persistently requesting that his problems be removed, learned the sufficiency of the grace of Christ. His weakness became his strength. In turn, he used this personal example to illustrate the power of Christ in a broad range of "weaknesses, insults, hardships, persecutions, and calamities."

This powerful example, regardless of any stoic strength Paul might otherwise have had as a person, is put in a christological context. Even so, it lends itself easily to a practical interpretation that will not allow suicide as an answer to human suffering.

To Be Content (Phil. 4:11-13)

Not that I complain of want; for I have learned, in whatever state I am, to be content. I know how to be abased, and I know how to abound; in any and all circumstances I have learned the secret of facing plenty and hunger, abundance and want. I can do all things in him who strengthens me.

Once more the emphasis is on endurance in the face of hardships, but always in the context of grace, not works. The author says explicitly earlier in his letter that his readers are to follow his example. Peace, grounded in God's grace, is to replace anxiety as they face the future.

Steadfastness and Faith (2 Thess. 1:4)

. . . we ourselves boast of you in the churches of God for your steadfastness and faith in all your persecutions and in all the afflictions which you are enduring.

By so commending and encouraging those who have endured persecution, Paul is seen here as reaffirming his own belief that voluntary martyrdom is not the desirable response to persecution. The remainder of the first chapter stresses the same concept of testing found in Job and in the apocalyptic works of Daniel and Revelation. Not only will those who survive the test "be made worthy of the kingdom of God" (v. 5), but they are assured that God will afflict those who now afflict Paul's readers in Thessalonica. Paul is not content to credit their endurance to mere human stoic steadfastness. To do that and no more would lead inevitably to reliance on their own good works and virtue. Rather, Paul adds the dimension of faith, relying upon the grace of God.

3

Does the Bible
Condone Suicide?

Who is really "for" suicide, except in the most unusual set of circumstances? I believe that to make an argument granting its permission
under some circumstances also carries with it the obligation to define,
as nearly as possible, the precise situations in which a person might
choose a self-inflicted or self-arranged death. Ethicists have sought
upon occasion to accept this burden of proof by showing that such
situations do, indeed, exist.

Condone, as used here, means "to pardon," "to excuse," or "not
to condemn" a specific act. The emphasis is on forgiving, rather than
on advocating the act. To condone is a far cry from arguing that
suicide be looked upon without concern. It is not an act that would
be intentionally encouraged. The following discussion has no such
intent. Rather, it is offered to help understand both why and how
certain biblical texts have been interpreted in ways that do not condemn suicide.

Some of the passages cited below may seem quite unrelated to
the subject of suicide. They reflect, however, the way many devout
people use the Bible to help them with their personal concerns. An
example of this came when I asked a student to submit a list of the
New Testament texts that had a bearing on suicide. I was not prepared
for the long number of passages he presented and asked how he had

gone about selecting them. At the time, the student was serving a
small rural church. He replied that one of his parishioners, an elderly
woman who had been active in the community and faithful in the
church for many years, had recently committed suicide. Looking back
over her life in the months preceding her death, friends recalled that
several times she had mentioned that she was "ready to go." In response to my question, the student said, "As I thought about her,
I read through the New Testament as if I were that woman, looking
for texts that would make me think it was all right to take my life
under her circumstances."

The texts used to condone suicide have been divided into
categories, according to various types of arguments. First are those
which give assurance that God will never forsake us. A second group
illustrates the rejection of the present age, regardless of the reasons.
A third group, though relatively few in number, contains texts seen
as specific commands to give up one's life for others. Finally, there
are biblical examples of self-sacrifice and of figures who expressed
suicidal tendencies.

GOD'S ABIDING LOVE FOR US

For centuries the church adhered to the doctrine that people who take
their own lives are immediately and eternally damned. Yet there are
biblical texts which clearly and without qualification assert the univer-
sality and eternal nature of God's love and grace.

God Is Everywhere (Ps. 139:8-10)

> If I ascend to heaven, thou art there!
> If I make my bed in Sheol, thou art there!
> If I take the wings of the morning
> and dwell in the uttermost parts of the sea,
> even there thy hand shall lead me,
> and thy right hand shall hold me.

No text in the Bible offers a more profound expression of the
assurance of God's unqualified love and presence. Its comfort has
sustained the faithful through centuries of the worst kinds of inward
and outward difficulties. Lacking any restrictions, it can easily be
read as a caveat to, if not outright refutation of, the idea that those

who commit suicide put themselves beyond the pale of God's love and care.

Forgiveness (Matt. 12:31; Mark 3:28-30; Luke 12:10)

Therefore I tell you, every sin and blasphemy will be forgiven men, but the blasphemy against the Holy Spirit will not be forgiven.

For those who might contemplate suicide, but are convinced they are faithful, such an act may not be seen as "blaspheming against the Holy Spirit." They would find these words reassuring, even if they did think suicide was one among other sins for which they would be forgiven.

Christ's Presence (Matt. 28:20b)

Lo, I am with you always, to the close of the age.

Although the closing words of Matthew's Gospel were addressed by Jesus to his disciples, they are in keeping with the general Christian notion that Christ is always present in the lives of the faithful.

Eternal Life (John 3:16)

For God so loved the world that he gave his only Son, that whoever believes in him should not perish but have eternal life.

For persons who truly believe in God's son, these words also could override the notion that suicide would cut them off from the Lord forever. The assurance of eternal life for believers is a common theme for John's readers (see also John 6:40; 17:1-3).

Resurrection of Life (John 5:28-29)

Do not marvel at this; for the hour is coming when all who are in the tombs will hear his voice and come forth, those who have done good, to the resurrection of life, and those who have done evil, to the resurrection of judgment.

Anyone not absolutely certain that they would go straight to hell for eternal damnation, and convinced they had done good things in and with their lives, could find comfort in these words when they thought about what would follow after their self-chosen death. The passage could be a source of even greater assurance for those who saw their suicide as a final expression of good for others.

No Condemnation (Rom. 8:1-2)

There is therefore now no condemnation for those who are in Christ Jesus. For the law of the Spirit of life in Christ Jesus has set me free from the law of sin and death.

This chapter has long been recognized as pivotal in the theology of Paul, summarizing a crucial section in his famous letter. The opening verses of the chapter, when viewed from the perspective of one convinced he or she was "in Christ Jesus," could provide further assurance that suicide would not bring condemnation.

Christ Is in You (Rom. 8:10-11)

But if Christ is in you, although your bodies are dead because of sin, your spirits are alive because of righteousness. If the Spirit of him who raised Jesus from the dead dwells in you, he who raised Christ Jesus from the dead will give life to your mortal bodies also through his Spirit which dwells in you.

For Christian believers preoccupied with their own sinfulness in the physical body, and with little hope of forsaking their ways, these words might well seem to offer a way out. That is, they could be taken as assurance that, by forsaking the sins of the flesh through suicide, one could indeed be alive to the Spirit. A sincere Christian caught up in the hellish tortures of alcoholism and drug abuse might use such words to make suicide appealing as a means of ending the misery suffered by themselves, their family, and their friends.

In Everything (Rom. 8:28)

We know that in everything God works for good with those who love him, who are called according to his purpose.

In the midst of disappointment, frustration, and doubt, these words could reinforce the trust of believers that God will bring good even out of their own suicide. To leave the results of such an act in God's hands, however, is to tread lightly with the suffering that such a death would bring to survivors. It is this last point that has received attention among recent ethical discussions (see chapter 5).

Failure to reflect carefully and sympathetically on the full impact of one's suicide on others is a major flaw in Christian moral judgment.

Nothing Can Separate Us (Rom. 8:38-39)

> For I am sure that neither death, nor life, nor angels, nor principalities, nor things present, nor things to come, nor powers, nor height, nor depth, nor anything else in all creation, will be able to separate us from the love of God in Christ Jesus our Lord.

In this passage, which really begins with verse 31, Paul is again using his characteristic exaggerated terms. It is this lack of qualification in his enthusiasm for the faith that has often led to misunderstanding among his followers and condemnation from his opponents. Nevertheless, in phrases expressing the same sublime thought as Psalm 139, Paul offers the ultimate assurance that "nothing . . . in all creation can separate us from the love of God." Given the thrust of his arguments in this famous chapter, it would seem entirely out of place for him to offer now any qualification to that strong, sure affirmation of hope.

We Are the Lord's (Rom. 14:7-12)

> None of us lives to himself, and none of us dies to himself. If we live, we live to the Lord, and if we die, we die to the Lord; so then, whether we live or whether we die, we are the Lord's. For to this end Christ died and lived again, that he might be Lord both of the dead and of the living.
> Why do you pass judgment on your brother? Or you, why do you despise your brother? For we shall all stand before the judgment seat of God; for it is written,
> "As I live, says the Lord, every knee shall bow to me,
> and every tongue shall give praise to God."
> So each of us shall give account of himself to God.

Two elements related to suicide are to be noted in this passage. First, there is the assurance that true believers belong to the Lord, whether they live or die. Suicides are not specifically excluded, nor is any particular form of death or life, regardless of how sinful the individual might be.

The second element concerns the easy inclination to judge others' actions, whether it be how they observe the day, whether they eat or abstain from eating, or how they live or die. Paul clearly condemns those who so quickly judge others' behavior in apparently trivial matters. By so doing they overlook the essential theological point Paul is making. Conceivably this passage might also come as a form of assurance to Christians contemplating suicide, in which case the final statement might be taken as a word of promise, rather than a threat.

At Home or Away (2 Cor. 5:1-10)

> For we know that if the earthly tent we live in is destroyed, we have a building from God, a house not made with hands, eternal in the heavens. Here indeed we groan, and long to put on our heavenly dwelling, so that by putting it on we may not be found naked. For while we are still in this tent, we sigh with anxiety; not that we would be unclothed, but that we would be further clothed, so that what is mortal may be swallowed up by life. He who has prepared us for this very thing is God, who has given us the Spirit as a guarantee.
>
> So we are always of good courage; we know that while we are at home in the body we are away from the Lord, for we walk by faith, not by sight. We are of good courage, and we would rather be away from the body and at home with the Lord. So whether we are at home or away, we make it our aim to please him. For we must all appear before the judgment seat of Christ, so that each one may receive good or evil, according to what he has done in the body.

Although speaking of himself with the so-called "editorial we," Paul does not exclude those who might choose to destroy "the earthly tent" for themselves. The entire discussion here may well presuppose continued life in the body, where Paul apparently chose to remain. But his use of the expression, "whether we are at home or away" suggests that the faithful might count on opportunities to please the Lord in either circumstance. The blurring of the distinction between the two realms could easily invite one to step across the otherwise great divide between physical and spiritual life.

The Blood of Jesus (1 John 1:5-7)

> This is the message we have heard from him and proclaim to you, that God is light and in him is no darkness at all. If we say we have fellowship with him while we walk in darkness, we lie and do not

live according to the truth; but if we walk in the light, as he is in the light, we have fellowship with one another, and the blood of Jesus his Son cleanses us from all sin.

The basic question is whether "walking in the light" and "having fellowship with one another" are precluded by a self-chosen death. While such an act would certainly bring these activities to an end, any wrongdoing could conceivably be overcome by the final assurance that "the blood of Jesus . . . cleanses us from all sin." If it does not, then one is left with the questionable notion that by our own action, the grace of God could be thwarted, a subject Paul discusses in broader historical perspectives in Romans 9-11.

In any event, the final clause of the passage has been used to offer assurance to countless thousands, quite apart from the moral prerequisites of proper walking and necessary fellowship. On the other hand, a faithful person who had obeyed such commands through a long life of service and fellowship might conclude that a choice to end life, in the midst of those desirable activities, would not preempt the divine cleansing.

Although the Bible has been the basic focus of our attention in the first three chapters, one comment on another literary source may be in order. John Wesley was not alone when, in making a point of doctrine or polity, he would turn to the Book of Common Prayer, often citing it right along with Scriptures.

When Dr. and Mrs. Henry Pitt Van Dusen chose to end their lives, after he had served with distinction as President of Union Theological Seminary in New York City, she left a poignant suicide note which ended with this prayer from that book so highly revered among millions of devout Christians from several denominations:

O Lamb of God that takest away the sins of the world,
have mercy upon us.
O Lamb of God that takest away the sins of the world,
grant us thy peace.

The Van Dusens seemed convinced that whatever sin might have been involved in their forthcoming suicides, it would have been forgiven by the Lamb of God they had loved and served through many years.

It should be obvious that persons needing assurance of God's love with regard to suicide could find it in the texts cited above. At the same time, such interpretation requires a particular method. Most of the statements are taken out of context and then expanded to include the act of taking one's own life. In this sense, the interpreters are but "pounding the gold," to use Donne's phrase, either to condone the act or to see it as one which does not need forgiveness at all. Yet it is clear why such assuring texts have been read in this way; readers are trying to avoid restrictions that would exclude persons who commit suicide.

The history of religious experience and the desire to emphasize the assurance of God's presence often appears concurrently with the conviction that this life, this "present evil age" as Paul called it, simply is not worth hanging on to. It is this category of texts condoning suicide that is now presented.

THE REJECTION OF THIS PRESENT AGE

Both Judaism and Christianity have in various ways stressed the rejection of the world. Several reasons for this rejection are: apocalyptic emphasis, a general worldview that deems this terrible age so corrupt that only God can redeem it; the individualized emphasis on the corruption and temptation of the flesh; and the gnostic or mystical teachings of a better, spiritual world into which the believer might enter. This rejection has at times become the basis for thinking that suicide was an acceptable way of removing oneself from a place of unrelieved evil, suffering, and shame to a place of eternal goodness and peace.

When You Are Old (John 21:18-19)

> Truly, truly, I say to you, when you were young, you girded yourself and walked where you would; but when you are old, you will stretch out your hands, and another will gird you and carry you where you do not wish to go.

"When you are old." The words have an all-too-painful ring for so many of the elderly. As the average age in America increases, the problems attendant to that demographic fact are enormous. Not the least of these pertains to the care and quality of life for individuals. The realism of Jesus' observation might lead those who read his words to conclude, "Surely he would understand."

Endurance in Hope (Rom. 8:18-23)

I consider that the sufferings of this present time not worth comparing with the glory that is to be revealed to us. For the creation waits with eager longing for the revealing of the sons of God; for the creation was subjected to futility, not of its own will but by the will of him who subjected it in hope; because the creation itself will be set free from its bondage to decay and obtain the glorious liberty of the children of God. We know that the whole creation has been groaning in travail until now; and not only the creation, but we ourselves, who have the first fruits of the Spirit, groan inwardly as we wait for adoption as sons, the redemption of our bodies.

In the midst of the same chapter in which appear several assurances of God's love, this passage describes the unworthiness of the world, this present age (the word *kosmos* in Greek could mean either or both) when compared to the one to come. Again the question arises, Does the individual have the right to choose the time, place, and method of moving from one place to another? For thousands of faithful believers, the answer has been an unequivocal yes. Some classic examples of this belief and action will be presented in chapter 4.

This passage is a very important one for understanding Paul's doctrine of Christian hope. Like many common terms in the New Testament, hope is used in several ways, some with very profound theological meaning. Paul goes on to write more about hope in verses 24 and 25, and seems to indicate that in spite of the difficulties life brings, our call is to endure and hope.

Do Not Love the World (1 John 2:15-17)

Do not love the world or the things in the world. If anyone loves the world, love for the Father is not in him. For all that is in the world, the lust of the flesh and the lust of the eyes and the pride of life, is not of the Father but is of the world. And the world passes away, and the lust of it; but he who does the will of God abides forever.

These words, used to denigrate the world, are harsh and unequivocal. They come from a writer within that segment of early Christianity known as the Johannine school, a setting where the church is withdrawn and exclusivistic. The tone is like that found throughout much of the Fourth Gospel and the three epistles accorded to John.

The faithful are here assured that the world with its temptations "passes away," while true believers abide. Even so, the more severe the rejection of the world, the easier it is to leave it for promised glory with the Lord.

Renunciation of This Life (John 12:25; Matt. 10:39; Mark 8:35; Luke 9:24; 14:26-27; 7:33)

He who loves his life loses it, and he who hates his life in this world will keep it for eternal life.

Given the general disregard for the world, these words could be taken as an encouragement to true believers to make sure that they did lose their lives, and so "gain" it by making the ultimate renunciation of this life.

A New Jerusalem (Rev. 21:1-5)

Then I saw a new heaven and a new earth; for the first heaven and the first earth had passed away, and the sea was no more. And I saw the holy city, new Jerusalem, coming down out of heaven from God, prepared as a bride adorned for her husband; and I heard a loud voice from the throne saying, "Behold, the dwelling of God is with men. He will dwell with them, and they shall be his people, and God himself will be with them; he will wipe away every tear from their eyes, and death shall be no more, neither shall there be mourning nor crying nor pain any more, for the former things have passed away."

Both Daniel and Revelation reflect that type of literary response to extreme persecution known as apocalypticism. From this perspective, the earth is so far beyond redemption that it has been totally written off by God. In its place is a new Jerusalem that will soon come to be inherited by those who remain faithful. Although there are specific exclusions—among them, for example, the cowardly, the faithless, and the polluted (see vs. 8)—we can see that one who considered herself or himself none of these, but truly one of the faithful, might intentionally and courageously express their faith by taking leave of a world so corrupt that even God would no longer have anything to do with it. This world is not to be redeemed, but entirely replaced!

In a variety of ways, then, the Bible has sometimes been interpreted as an outright condemnation of this world. When taken to extremes, this rejection has made the choice of suicide easier, and conceivably even put it within the realm of religious devotion. An even stronger enticement to such action has occasionally come from texts which some read as specific commands to leave this world.

THE CALL TO MARTYRDOM AND SELF-SACRIFICE

Recall here what was said in the introduction about a definition of suicide. While many would not consider the giving of one's life in the midst of persecution suicide, but only the ultimate expression of faithfulness, others, from Augustine on, have rejected the act even under those "heroic" circumstances. The need for careful definition applies also to any self-sacrifice on behalf of others.

When at the beginning of World War II Colin P. Kelly chose to crash his bomber into an enemy warship, he became the first person of that conflict to receive the Medal of Honor. The history of virtually every race, nation, and creed has such heroes. Those who choose to take their own lives to bear witness to their faith, to support a cause (either offensively, like Samson, or defensively, like Ignatius), to save others, or merely to make life better for them, may thus, for purposes of discussion, be considered suicides.

To omit examples of and references to such behavior would be to omit important dimensions of this discussion. Self-chosen deaths, regardless of motive, should be included in the definition of suicide, as was stated in the introduction to this book. This reminder will be especially important in considering the examples given in this category of texts condoning suicide.

The Deaths of Zebah and Zalmun'na (Judg. 8:18-21)

Then he (Gideon) said to Zebah and Zalmun'na, "Where are the men whom you slew at Tabor?" They answered, "As you are, so were they, every one of them; they resembled the sons of a king." And he said, "They were my brothers, the sons of my mother; as the Lord lives, if you had saved them alive, I would not slay you." And he said to Jether his first-born, "Rise and slay them." But the youth did not draw his sword; for he was afraid, because he was still a youth. Then Zebah and Zalmun'na said, "Rise yourself, and fall upon us; for as the man is, so is his strength." And Gideon arose and slew Zebah and Zalmun'na.

It is difficult under any circumstances to consider this particular request as a suicide in the same way as the one mentioned in chapter 1 concerning Abimelech (Judg. 9:52-54). But the account is an example of a unique dimension of death in ancient historiography. According to Newell, Josephus and other historians of his day frequently described the defeated enemies of military heroes in noble light, seeking to enhance even further the stature of their principle figure. The more honorable the slain, the more honorable the slayer. What we have here reflects that type of historical reporting with its particular interest in Gideon.[1]

As for the request, the sneering rebuke of Zebah and Zalmun'na to Gideon, they knew their deaths were imminent. They felt no apparent disgrace over who killed them, as did Abimelech. Nor did they seem to have an altruistic motive, as did Jonah. They had even more reason to expect death for their action than the Philippian jailer. For whatever reason, there was a clear, intentional decision behind their statement to have Gideon himself "fall upon" them.

Our God Will Deliver Us (Dan. 3:16-18)

Shadrach, Meshach, and Abed'nego answered the king, "O Nebuchad-nez'zar, we have no need to answer you in this matter. If it be so, our God whom we serve is able to deliver us from the fiery furnace; and he will deliver us out of your hand, O king. But if not, be it known to you, O king, that we will not serve your gods or worship the golden image which you have set up.

The encouragement of the faithful to hold on, to bear up under persecution and not recant, is a primary concern of apocalyptic literature. One of the best ways to elicit such steadfastness is to tell of those who have exhibited such faithfulness. Indeed, the worse the persecution described, and the more steadfast the hero, the more impressive the story is likely to be on the readers who might be weakening in their faith.

In a time of severe persecution, the author of the book of Daniel told the story of heroes of the faith. Three Jews were informed that they would be burned in a fiery furnace if they did not renounce their faith. Their defiant refusal, and their noble reply to the king himself, is a classic expression of religious faith: Our God is able to deliver us. Our God will deliver us. But if not. . . .

Happily, God did deliver them, but the readers would no doubt know of many who had not survived similar ordeals. The call to martyrdom has its roots in stories such as this, even though the endings shift the focus from deliverance in this life to promises of an eternal life in a better world. Thus, a willingness to die for the faith leads to martyrdom and all its rewards. As we shall see in chapter 4, the time came when many Christians were all too eager to achieve martyrdom by forcing death upon themselves.

The Gospel of Mark has received much renewed attention in recent years with regard to date, its relationship to Matthew and Luke, its theology, and its literary construction. The results have produced a variety of conclusions, but from a theological, historical, and literary perspective, the purpose of Mark is now often referred to as "a call to martyrdom." Other gospels seem to be less intent on confronting the reader with the decision of whether or not to lay down one's life as a sign of faithfulness. Several passages in Mark are now seen as pointing clearly in this direction.

Call to Martyrdom (Mark 8:34-35)

> And he called to him the multitude with his disciples, and said to them, "If any man would come after me, let him deny himself and take up his cross and follow me. For whoever would save his life will lose it; and whoever would lose his life for my sake and the gospel's will save it."

Jesus' call to self-denial, to taking up one's cross, and to losing one's life in order to save it, are mentioned six times in the four Gospels. (See also Matt. 10:39; Luke 9:24; 14:26-27; 17:33; John 12:25.) Through the centuries they have prompted innumerable acts of selfless courage. In the context of Mark's Gospel, they emphasize the necessity of putting a low priority on the value of one's own life when it comes to a choice between maintaining that life at all costs and bearing faithful witness to Jesus Christ. Thus life itself could more easily be dispensed with in order to serve others in Christ's name.

A significant difference is to be noted between Mark's recording of Jesus' words and those which appear in Luke 9:23. In terms of form-critical research, Luke's addition in recording "take up his cross daily" suggests that Luke was writing for a different audience, one for whom Jesus' call to martyrdom and death would have become only a daily, on-going form of self-sacrifice. Yet, in Luke 14:27, the word "daily" is not used, nor does it occur in Matthew 10:38-39.

To Give His Life (Mark 10:42-45)

And Jesus called them to him and said to them, "You know that those who are supposed to rule over the Gentiles lord it over them, and their great men exercise authority over them. But it shall not be so among you; but whoever would be great among you must be your servant, and whoever would be first among you must be slave of all. For the Son of man also came not to be served but to serve, and to give his life as a ransom for the many."

The last verse could be taken as one which merely supports Jesus as an example of one who gave his life for others. Putting aside the question of whether or not Jesus himself committed suicide, as some have claimed, it is significant that the statement occurs at the conclusion of a specific commandment to James and John and, through the literary intention of the author, to all of Mark's readers. The statement may not be read simply as an example, but as an injunction to follow a way of life that leads to martyrdom.

The terrible realities awaiting the faithful are presented graphically in Mark 13, often referred to as "the little apocalypse." In perilous times the faithful are called to steadfast witness, even when it means giving up their lives. If and when persecution comes, they are to remember Jesus' example as well as his words, "I have told you all things beforehand."

In Times of Oppression (Luke 23:28-31)

But Jesus turning to them, said, "Daughters of Jerusalem, do not weep for me, but weep for yourselves and for your children. For behold, the days are coming when they will say, 'Blessed are the barren, and the wombs that never bore, and the breasts that never gave suck!' Then they will begin to say to the mountains, 'Fall on us'; and to the hills, 'Cover us.' For if they do this when the wood is green, what will happen when it is dry?"

Jesus' prediction of evil days, expressly given to the women who were following him along the *Via Dolorosa*, includes the vision of their crying out for natural calamities to take their lives. These, according to Luke, were Jesus' last words before the crucifixion.

It would be difficult to think of Jesus, at that crucial moment, condemning the women who might offer such pleas. In keeping with Luke's characteristic portrayal of Jesus as one constantly concerned for the marginalized in society, it is more likely that the intent of these words was to express his typical selfless concern for the suffering of others, even on his way to the cross! By so announcing the coming woe in these terms, Jesus was not condemning the desire for death in times of oppression. (See Luke 21:23-24; for similar words that apply to the enemy, see Rev. 6:15-17.)

Lay Down Your Life (John 15:12-14)

This is my commandment, that you love one another as I have loved you. Greater love has no man than this, that a man lay down his life for his friends. You are my friends if you do what I command you.

The greatest of all commandments is to love. The giving of one's life for another is here expressly declared by Jesus to be the greatest expression of love. No follower of his can be uncertain about this call to self-sacrifice. Jesus was clearly referring to himself as the one about to die for his friends (v. 13), but he was also serving as a model for them, so that he did not mean to exclude their dying for family or for faith.

The extent to which one goes to obey such a command and the question of whether or not the motive is genuine altruistic love, as opposed to personal gain, are questions that must ultimately be answered according to individual conscience. But with such a forceful statement before us, the primary concern for other people (family, friends, and even foes) must take precedence in our daily lives, regardless of how the questions of inward motive may finally be answered.

Suffering to Make the Gospel Known (Acts 20:22-24)

And now, behold, I am going to Jerusalem, bound in the Spirit, not knowing what shall befall me there; except that the Holy Spirit testifies to me in every city that imprisonment and afflictions await me. But I do not account my life of any value nor as precious to myself, if only I may accomplish my course and the ministry which I have received from the Lord Jesus, to testify to the gospel of the grace of God.

Characteristic of his biographical account in Acts, Paul is depicted as a genuine hero of the faith, one who has already suffered in order that the gospel might be made known throughout the world. Here, in a statement of how he views his own life in relationship to that ministry, his biographer presents a point of view that was intended to be accepted by the early church. Regardless of the hardships ahead, personal safety and self-preservation are always subjugated to one's ministry to others in the name of Christ.

Perhaps for a Good Person (Rom. 5:7)

> Why, one will hardly die for a righteous man – though perhaps for a good man one will dare even to die.

As difficult and rare as the case may be, Paul affirms that one may give one's life for a good person and do it without condemnation. Although the comment is made in the context of one of Paul's most profound christological statements, its practical value is not to be overlooked. In arguing his theological positions, Paul often drew upon human experience for illustrations and support. But he could never rightfully be accused of using experiences he disagreed with in order to convince his readers of the arguments he was trying to make.

But Have Not Love (1 Cor. 13:3)

> If I give away all that I have, and if I deliver my body to be burned, but have not love, I gain nothing.

At least three problems attend this verse. What was the original text? What did Paul mean? How does it relate to the matter of voluntary (self-giving) martyrdom?

Several recent English translations note that an alternate reading, found in a number of manuscripts, is "deliver my body that I may glory." In the New Oxford Annotated Bible, John Knox commented that this variant reading:

> Probably represents an ancient attempt to avoid what might be regarded as an absurdity: How could one accept a martyr's death unless one is moved by love? But Paul knows that pride or perverted self-interest can conceivably move one to make such a sacrifice.[2]

Even the reading of the King James Version, retained in the Revised Standard Version (with the variant reading given in a note) has been understood in different ways. Some take it to mean a willingness, even eagerness, to have one's own body burned at the stake. Such a practice, however, is more akin to Medieval inquisitions and intrachurch wars than to first-century persecution by the Romans. Others have suggested the burning to mean branding, as when one would give oneself to a new master. This theory has not been widely accepted, partly because it tends to lessen the force of Paul's argument. The explicit qualification, "and have not love," could be, and no doubt often was, waived by those convinced that they were expressing such love at the moment they "gave their bodies." They could, without considering themselves perverted or filled with pride, do so with the assurance that the apostle would have approved. At times, bodies were given when the state really did not want them, thus causing a problem for the church (see chapter 4).

Assuming that the reference is to the voluntary giving of one's life, the text would support the idea that such action, when done in love, was acceptable. Fedden was convinced that this verse in itself must have been a justification to numberless Christians who compelled the state to take their lives. It was an approach to grace, he noted, no less worthy, but equally as ineffectual, as almsgiving and eloquence.[3]

Despairing of Life (2 Cor. 1:8)

> For we do not want you to be ignorant, brethren, of the affliction we experienced in Asia; for we were so utterly, unbearably crushed that we despaired of life itself.

Paul openly admits that because of almost unbearable hardships, the desire to live had at times escaped him, and he does so without suggesting that it was immoral for him to feel the way he did. But he goes on to show that he and his companions of the Way were rescued by God and that such a delivery became the basis for his hope that God would do so again. Thus, while it is good to be rescued from the despair of life, simply to have the despair is, in itself, not immoral. In this passage he was stressing the severity of the affliction, not confessing his sin. This would strongly suggest that those who have such thoughts deserve empathy and help more than censure.

Elusive Death (Rev. 9:6)

And in those days men will seek death and will not find it; they will long to die, and death will fly from them.

The ghastly prediction of the fifth angel was directed against those "who have not the seal of God upon their foreheads." As in Revelation 6:16, the desire to flee this life without the ability to do so is a mark of the extreme torture which the unrighteous are to receive. Implied in this description of what awaits the wicked is the contrast, namely, that if the righteous should make such a plea, it would be granted. At least there is no condemnation of the righteous if they should desire to see their lives end.

One reason people could more easily condone suicide is by interpreting passages like the above as specific commands to give their lives willingly, either as a witness to the faith or as a self-sacrifice for others. Such passages might also suggest to them that the desire to see their lives ended would be neither immoral nor a breach of faith.

EXAMPLES OF SUICIDAL BEHAVIOR
AND SELF-SACRIFICE

The repeated calls to self-sacrifice and martyrdom expressed by several of the New Testament writers show how easily genuine believers could be led to sacrifice themselves, either on behalf of others or as a demonstration of their "last full measure of devotion" to Christ, or both.

Another reason why those who read the Bible might see suicide as an act not to be condemned is the number of persons who either took or gave their lives for a noble cause, or who expressed suicidal thoughts without being condemned for it. That is, in addition to specific words, there were examples.

We have already noted in chapter 1 the suicidal prayers of Samson and Jonah, one granted and the other frustrated. These examples, plus the intervention of Paul into the suicide attempt of the Philippian jailer, show that suicidal behavior in the New Testament was far from unknown. It is even more widely recognized, however, in further instances of suicidal behavior, even though they did not result in specific attempts.

Eli'jah (1 Kgs. 19:4)

> But he himself [Eli'jah] went a day's journey into the wilderness, and came and sat down under a broom tree; and he asked that he might die, saying, "It is enough; now O Lord, take away my life; for I am no better than my fathers."

The despondency and fear that gripped Eli'jah led him to flee Jez'ebel and go into the wilderness alone. There he offered his prayer for God to take his life because he had been unable, like his fathers, to root out the idolatry that had come upon his people.

Although Eli'jah was not condemned for wanting to end his life, God did take him to task for wallowing in self-pity. It was a sign of God's faithfulness and knowledge of what could yet be accomplished through Eli'jah. The confrontation in the cave, resulting in Eli'jah's hearing the "still small voice," led to God's command for the prophet to stop feeling sorry for himself and start going about the work of the Lord again, specifically in the political life of the nation: "Go, return on your way to the wilderness of Damascus; and when you arrive, you shall anoint Haz'ael to be king over Syria. . ." (1 Kgs. 19:15).

Jonah (Jon. 4:3, 9)

> Therefore now, O Lord, take my life from me, I beseech thee, for it is better for me to die than to live.
>
> . . .
>
> But God said to Jonah, "Do you do well to be angry for the plant?" And he said, "I do well to be angry, angry enough to die."

Jonah's suicidal tendencies have been noted by the seventeenth-century English cleric John Donne, as well as by the Nobel Prize-winning Jewish author Elie Wiesel in our own day. Donne noted that in spite of this designation of Jonah as having attempted suicide, Saint Jerome called him "Saint Jonah," and Nicholas of Lyra considered him holy. In centuries-old icons, Jonah is depicted with the traditional holy aura about his head. Donne concluded, "Thus we may esteem him [Jonah] advised, ordinate, and rectified in all these approaches that he made by wishing and assenting to his own death."[4]

Estimations of Jonah may vary, but there is no indication that his expressed wishes to die, or even his attempt to do so, were in themselves condemned.

Paul (Acts 21:12-14)

When we heard this, we and the people there begged him not to go up to Jerusalem. Then Paul answered, "What are you doing, weeping and breaking my heart? For I am ready not only to be imprisoned but even to die at Jerusalem for the name of the Lord Jesus." And when he would not be persuaded, we ceased and said, "The will of the Lord be done."

According to his biographer in the book of Acts, Paul was always willing, if necessary, to die for the faith. Fear was no deterrent to going wherever he felt called, even though it would surely mean his death. Once his resolve was deemed to be firm, it was accepted by his fellow Christians.

To Live or Die (Phil. 1:21-24)

For me to live is Christ, and to die is gain. If it is to be life in the flesh, that means fruitful labor for me. Yet which I shall choose I cannot tell. I am hard pressed between the two. My desire is to depart and be with Christ, for that is far better. But to remain in the flesh is more necessary on your account.

Paul was aware of the possibility of his own death as a result of his ministry. His own perils, recorded so graphically in 2 Corinthians, and at least one successful attempt to escape capture and possible death (Acts 9:23-25), are sufficient proof of this. But the statement in this passage concerning his knowledge that "to die is gain" does not come as the result of despair or fear of death. His success in the past, his hope for the future, his confidence that God's grace was sufficient in the present, are unquestioned. The striking comment here is not that he is free to choose (v. 22), but that quite frankly he has not yet made up his mind which course of action he will take! He concludes (v. 24) that for the sake of others he will continue to labor.

Although the church would never have been the same had Paul chosen an early death, the point is that he had no immediate sense of wrong-doing in contemplating his self-chosen death: "which I shall choose I cannot tell."

These passages show a lack of condemnation toward expressed suicidal wishes. Also pointing in this direction are the large number of laws in the Hebrew Bible and the so-called "vice-lists" of the New Testament, none of which expressly condemned suicide. This fact is, in itself, somewhat surprising. It may explain why several centuries of biblical writers had to go with a rather broad interpretation of the commandment against murder in order to explain the lack of condemnation of suicide anywhere else in the Bible. An equally surprising fact is that later biblical writers never once referred to the commandment in terms of prohibiting suicide.

Several scholars have given special attention to the vice lists in Christian literature. In his commentary on *The Pastoral Epistles*, Hans Conzelmann noted that among the vices listed in 1 Timothy 1:8-11, 2 Timothy 3:2-5, Romans 1:28-32, and Jude 16, most came from common lists already well-known and accepted in the societies of the Hellenistic world of Paul's day. The same may also be said for the several lists of virtues that usually accompanied the lists of evil deeds.

The lack of any specific condemnation of suicide leads us to conclude that the biblical writers simply gave no serious thought to the issue, even though suicidal acts and tendencies were clearly in evidence.

TEXTS CONDONING SELF-SACRIFICE

A few texts may be taken as examples of either a willingness to give one's life or a specific command to do so. Again, it is well to keep in mind that the precise formula for doing so is not spelled out in the Bible. This omission has left later generations to wrestle with the attendant practical problems of when, where, how, and whether to give one's life in specific situations.

The Good Shepherd (John 10:11-15)

I am the good shepherd. The good shepherd lays down his life for the sheep. He who is a hireling and not a shepherd, whose own the sheep are not, sees the wolf coming and leaves the sheep and flees; and the wolf snatches them and scatters them. He flees because he is a hireling and cares nothing for the sheep. I am the good shepherd; I know my own and my own know me, as the Father knows me and I know the Father; and I lay down my life for the sheep.

These verses are so explicit they need little comment. In John's view, Jesus is the one who voluntarily laid down his life for those he loved.

Jesus, now the reigning Christ (again, in John's view), complicates the issue with his comments that once he has laid down his life, he then has the power to take it up again (v. 18). But even so, the preceding verses can easily be taken as the example intended for his followers, even though they did not share his suprahuman power.

Peter and Thomas (John 13:37)

> Peter said to him, "Lord, why cannot I follow you now? I will lay down my life for you."

This is a specific example of a disciple offering to lay down his life for Jesus. Although it heightens the effect of Jesus' immediate prediction of Peter's subsequent denial of him, there is no hint that the offer to die for Jesus was itself condemned by the Lord. A similar statement is made in John 11:16, when Thomas, the Twin, says, "Let us also go [with Jesus], that we may die with him."

By This We Know Love (1 John 3:16)

> By this we know love, that he laid down his life for us; and we ought to lay down our lives for the brethren.

Moving a step beyond mere example, this specific injunction is based squarely on Jesus' having laid down his life rather than having had it taken from him. The extent to which Christians ought to lay down their lives through a self-managed death, as well as the ways in which such an act might be carried out, are practical matters to be determined by every follower of Christ in every age. There can be little doubt, however, that genuine faith, informed by this understanding of Jesus' example and coupled with this clear injunction, has supported thousands of Christian martyrs in making that difficult and reluctant decision.

This long chapter on texts used to condone suicide shows that there are a large number of texts on the subject. This must not, however, be taken as evidence that the biblical writers were overwhelmingly in favor of suicide. They simply show, as stated at the beginning of this chapter, that a larger number of texts may be *interpreted* as condoning suicide than many would have supposed. Some of the biblical statements seem supportive of suicide to devout Christians, many of whom did choose that way of death in the early centuries of the church. It is not too surprising, then, that equally devout Christians today may make a similar interpretation of those same texts.

CONCLUSION

Perhaps it will seem disappointing that this detailed look at more than seventy biblical texts leaves us with a conclusion that others have noted earlier. But the problem of finding a clear, unequivocal position in the whole Bible on most any subject is never an easy task — often an impossible one. Such is the pluralism inherent in the Bible itself. Bailey, in *Biblical Perspectives on Death*, says further:

> It is difficult to recover a clear, systematic perspective on death in the writings of Matthew, Mark, and Luke, in part because they have used a number of earlier sources and in part because the topic is seldom directly addressed.[5]

> It is precarious to speak of *the* biblical response to death. Rather, there is a variety of responses, depending upon the time and circumstance. Nevertheless, some views tend to predominate, to endure, or to have a common denominator.[6]

In referring to the current ethical problems of when to withdraw life-support systems, a problem often discussed by ancient physicians, even without our degree of high technology, Bailey also noted that:

> Perhaps the most that can be said is that the issue . . . is an ambiguous one, and that the Bible is an accurate reflection of that ambiguity.[7]

In spite of such inconclusiveness about the topic of death, the exercise has not been without its unique values. First, this broad survey has put together in one place the largest number of texts related to that subject. It has also divided the texts into two major types of evidence, direct and indirect. This in itself provides a framework for understanding "what the Bible says" on the subject. As for the direct accounts, the study gives close attention to familiar texts (e.g., those concerning Saul, Samson, Jonah, and Judas) as well as the numerous texts providing indirect evidence. The indirect texts, both condemnations and condonations, have been further sub-divided to show the types of arguments which have influenced the interpretations of those texts.

The next step in the review of suicide texts is to look at several ways the biblical texts have been interpreted throughout history. This will include a brief look at types of current biblical criticism, especially the interpretations of Saul as a suicide. Both subjects are important for anyone seeking to use the Bible in making personal and social ethical decisions related to suicide, simply because the texts are only as helpful as the ways in which one interprets them. Knowing the variety of interpretations in the past helps us to see the way we are making our own interpretation.

4

The Biblical Evidence
in History

The preceding chapters have identified and examined briefly more than seventy texts that either describe attempted and completed suicides or which have been used to condemn or condone those acts. Too often, a supposed belief in what the Bible originally said arose only centuries later, and has often been disputed, without current Bible lovers even being aware of it. The present chapter focuses on ways in which the Bible has been used, or neglected, at different times in history to inform religious communities on suicide. It seeks to provide modern interpreters with a broad perspective when addressing the issue of suicide. Because of its focus on a limited topic for investigation, this chapter is unique among the many accounts of the history of suicide. Besides Fedden's classic work, only a few helpful summaries are available.[1] None of these, however, gives primary attention to biblical interpretation, although several make passing reference to it when commenting on the teachings of the church.

THE IMPORTANCE OF HISTORICAL PERSPECTIVE

Historical perspective is essential to achieving a clear understanding of one's own approach to the Bible. Much of what passes for new interpretation is really quite old. Errors of fact, mistakes of judgment, limitations of vision, and the need for charity are often forgotten. When individuals or communities use the Bible for personal faith and ethical decision making today, their conclusions will always be short-sighted without a careful look at the history of exegesis.

Interwoven with this survey are specific interpretations of Saul as a suicide, including a section on the broad range of views among Jewish thinkers, both past and present, a brief look at recent commentary on Saul, and a discussion of two very old but persistent problems.

It was noted above that biblical interpretation begins in the Bible itself. Few subjects, whether doctrinal or ethical, are presented consistently from Genesis to Revelation. For example, Paul is often spoken of in terms of his "development" of thought during his ministry. This fact underlies any history of exegesis, but is often overlooked. It is thus undervalued by many who place a primacy on Scripture as the source of their religious life and thought.

The recent approach to biblical study known as canonical criticism gives primary attention to the changes that occurred within the canon itself. To observe closely the ways in which biblical writers often reinterpreted earlier texts makes it easier to understand why commentators in later periods also gave new meanings to old words. This new critical approach has both relied upon and enhanced the significance of recent applications of sociological studies to the biblical word.

In chapter 1 the differing literary, historical, theological, and ethical implications of Saul in 1 Samuel 31, 2 Samuel 1, 2, and 10, and 1 Chronicles 10 were noted. Also observed was that in the early centuries of the church, most writers saw no need to comment on suicide. Self-chosen death, either by one's own hand or by the hand of another, was viewed as falling within acceptable, and at times honored Judeo–Christian behavior.

Variations in biblical interpretation are due, in part, to the constant changes that occurred within the church or society. Societal changes often affect the thinking of religious communities in profound ways. War, plagues, economics, technological advances, demographic shifts – all have affected biblical interpretation at least as much as theological insight, new forms of criticism, and textual and archaeological discoveries.

Less frequently, but still obvious, religious thought has affected vast areas of the world and the history of its people. The spread of major world religions, while never unaccompanied by a host of social forces, attests to this unquestioned fact. The world as we know it simply would not be the same had it not been for the Jewish prophetic movement, Christian evangelism, Buddhist teachings, and Islamic zeal, to name only the most obvious examples.

In tracing the history of exegesis in texts related to suicide, we must be equally aware of changes prompted by new religious views, and, wherever possible, we must show the interrelationship between religion and other dimensions of society. Although that relationship cannot always be clearly delineated, no aspect of society is ever totally unaffected by the others.

Two Roman Catholic scholars, Jacques Pohier and Dietmar Mieth, have recently affirmed the necessity of this awareness for valid theological and ethical reflection on suicide:

> These socio-cultural modifications in the meaning of death and its context have repercussions on the very ancient, but, alas, always contemporary problem of suicide. Important though the psychological factors in suicide may be, it remains true that socio-cultural factors are of decisive significance. Every socio-cultural change in our relationship with death alters the way in which individuals understand their right over their own death, and the right of society to require them to go on living.[2]

With these necessary considerations in mind, we may now look at some of the later periods of history in which religious communities interpreted biblical texts as they confronted suicide.

REJECTIONS OF SUICIDE BEFORE AUGUSTINE

In the collection of early Christian writings known as the Apostolic Fathers (C.E. 96-150), there are no explicit condemnations of suicide. The writings of Ignatius (see chapter 1) and Polycarp, and the account of Polycarp's martyrdom, go far to make self-chosen death for genuinely pious reasons a goal to which Christians might well aspire.

Eusebius had many good things to say about Christian martyrs in his *Ecclesiastical History*. Even Chrysostom extolled the virtues of martyrdom, particularly that of Pelagia, who took her life rather than be violated by her captors. Ambrose also concurred in attributing honor to those who exhibited true faith and love for others in dying by their own hand.

The major biblical bases for pre-Augustinian condemnations were a belief that suicide was homicide and that suicide was to be despised because that was the way the betrayer of Jesus behaved. The act of suicide thus suffered a kind of guilt by association with Judas. Augustine is generally acknowledged as the first to use "thou shalt not kill" as a specific prohibition against suicide,[3] but another early fourth century writer, Lactanius, said "For if a homicide is guilty because he is a destroyer of man, he who puts himself to death is under the same guilt, because he puts to death a man."[4]

Some positive responses were made to those who chose death for reasons of piety and martyrdom, but few specific texts were singled out to justify such instances, and apparently none when suicide occurred for less noble motives.

FROM AUGUSTINE TO AQUINAS

The impact of Augustine's polemic against suicide, made at a time when an impressive number of Christians were taking their own lives, solidified the church's thought against the act. His arguments were not limited to scriptural proofs alone. Indeed, most of them relied on rational arguments unattached to biblical justification. He did not allow accounts of suicide in Hebrew Scripture to be a cause of pious imitation.

Augustine's attacks came largely in response to the heretical Donatists, and their more radical sub-group, the Circumcellions, who strongly encouraged suicide as the ultimate act of piety. His primary concern was thus quite narrow. Many of the reasons which prompt suicide, such as emotional suffering, loss of dignity due to old age, personal or national honor and altruism, were not seriously considered. His arguments were drawn primarily from classical virtues and common sense, that is, what seemed most rational, coupled with the charge that the heretics were both selfish and full of pride. They were more concerned with their own welfare than they were in distributing charity to others.

Among the texts Augustine referred to were Ezekiel 18:31-32 and Matthew 4:5-7 (Luke 4:9-12). His most direct use of Scripture, however, was the interpretation of the commandment "Thou shalt not kill" to include self-killing. By so doing, he put firmly into place a cornerstone on which the condemnation of suicide was to last even to the present.

Although some important Christians of the early centuries did not disapprove of suicide, among them Tertullian and Valerian, in the centuries following Augustine the church in different locations took a series of steps to make suicide totally objectionable.

One unexpected fact in a close look at the development of the church's attitude toward suicide is the use of analogy between it and self-mutilation. This act was strictly forbidden for both clergy and laity. It was considered a form of aggression against the sanctity of human life and thus directly akin to homicide. It was perhaps on the basis of this reasoning that the condemnation of suicide first came into common law.

Other early conciliar developments occurred at Guadix (305), Carthage (348), and Braga (363). These councils successively: (1) purged from the list of martyrs all those who had taken their own lives; (2) condemned those who had taken their lives for personal reasons under the pretext of piety; and (3) condemned and denied proper rites of burial to all known suicides. In 806 Pope Nicholas I reaffirmed the order regarding burial, citing as biblical justification for his condemnation the death of Judas, and the Second Lateran Council (1129) also reiterated the traditional view. Blásquez's summary shows the widening ecclesiastical rejection of suicide from the time of Augustine, as well as the deeper reflections on motive, circumstance, and penalties.

A survey of these decrees, which worked their way into Roman Catholic canon law and remained virtually unchanged until 1983, shows that almost no attention was given to any biblical justification for the church's severe punishment of suicide among its members. This position, well entrenched from the time of Augustine, received even stronger support in the work of Thomas Aquinas.

FROM AQUINAS TO THE SIXTEENTH CENTURY

When Augustine attacked suicide, it was in response to a very specific crisis, that of rampant suicide among Christians. To make matters worse, the evil was being aided and abetted by a rising heretical movement. It was an evil that had serious practical implications for the church. Augustine followed the method sometimes employed by Paul and attempted to root out an evil practice by refuting the heretical theology from which it sprang.

Aquinas, on the other hand, seems to have been motivated by quite a different concern. Some nine hundred years later, he was writing not to root out a heresy or to stop the surge of suicidal behavior, but to complete his *Summa Theologiae*, a comprehensive systematic summation of Christian theology. He put the whole of Christian teaching on a new intellectual basis, grounded in the thought of Aristotle. He asked every question that he thought might be raised about the faith, then answered it in rigorous, systematic fashion. In dealing with the matter of human life, and the sin of destroying it, Aquinas was naturally led to address the issue of homicide and only then of suicide.

Only two of his four basic arguments can be considered biblically based. He agreed with Augustine that suicide is a violation of the Commandment, and he argued that it is a sin against the God of all creation who bestowed the gift of life upon human beings.

Although his reasons were both more philosophical and less practically oriented, Aquinas succeeded in nailing down even more tightly the Western church's official position against suicide, one which was to go unchallenged until the Renaissance.

SUICIDE AND THE REFORMERS

Toward the end of the Middle Ages a new intellectual movement began to exert its force on society. It took the form of a radical questioning and, in many instances, a total rejection of both earlier assumptions and ways of thinking. Centuries-old ideas about the world, humanity, government, and about the church and its teachings were challenged. People throughout Europe embraced a new birth of personal responsibility for their lives, individually and collectively. This new regard for the rights of every human being was at the center of Renaissance thought, and has had a continuing influence on society's customs and its laws.

As with most major intellectual and social movements, it is not easy to give specific times and places for their origins. For centuries, however, historians have looked back on the Renaissance as a movement covering the period roughly from the fourteenth through the sixteenth centuries. (The dates are still debated among historians.)

Of significance is the impact of this intellectual movement on the whole of society and how it affected the church. Much has been written on the relationship between the Renaissance and the Reformation, a time when some rather mundane economic and political forces combined with profound theological reasoning, effective proclamation, and bold ecclesiastical leadership set the church on an entirely new course. Luther, Calvin, and Zwingli on the continent, and Henry VIII, Archbishop Cranmer, and John Knox in England and Scotland all affected the political, social, theological, and ecclesiastical fabric of Western society in ways that have continued to the present.

With regard to suicide it is not difficult to see that a new emphasis on the meaning of life for the individual and one's own personal responsibility, coupled with a rejection of church authority would have an effect on the rights of individuals to choose how, when, and under what circumstances to end their lives. Two immediate questions are: Did attitudes toward suicide actually change? How was the Bible used either to condemn or condone suicide?

The extreme social stigma against suicide had reached its height in the Middle Ages. There was punishment for those who attempted it, public desecration of the corpses of those who committed it, and loss of inheritance and continuing social pressures for family survivors. (Today, stigma is generally regarded by suicidologists as both a reason for people not seeking the help they need to prevent suicide, as well as an unjust and often cruel form of punishment against innocent survivors.) Without exception, the leading Reformers continued to argue against suicide, usually for the reasons that had long been accepted.

It is somewhat surprising that, for all the emphasis on the new humanism fostered by the Renaissance and the new freedom proclaimed in Reformation theology, attitudes toward suicide remained virtually unchanged in both society and church. To be sure, Luther was apparently willing to express a different view, at least to his intimates, but the negative position remained firm, and no new interpretations of Scripture appeared.[5]

It would be misleading to conclude, however, that the strong intellectual force of these movements, particularly of the Renaissance, have had no lasting effect. Many Protestant churches today trace their roots more directly to the Renaissance than to the Reformation. The final evaluation of the impact of the Renaissance upon attitudes toward suicide, and to the way biblical interpretation has been changed by it, must go beyond the Reformation to still later centuries.

SEVENTEENTH- AND EIGHTEENTH-CENTURY INTERPRETATION

It must not be supposed that all biblical interpretation occurs within the closely guarded confines of the church or other official religious institutions. In any free society, where individual writers and artists are at liberty to express their creative inspiration, much of their grounding in the Bible will be evident. Whether that biblical understanding comes through rigorous biblical study, or is merely absorbed from a culture that has been influenced by it, poets, dramatists, painters, and sculptors create their own forms of biblical hermeneutics.

This point is nowhere more obvious than in the works of Shakespeare (1564–1616). The popularity of his plays in the late sixteenth and early seventeenth centuries make them primary historical and social documents for the study of English thought, values, and behavior.

Several of his greatest works—*Julius Caesar*, *Romeo and Juliet*, *Othello*, *Hamlet*—show that he and his audience considered suicide a fit subject for dramatic interpretation. Some of his best known characters chose their deaths by poison, sword, or drowning. The blinded Gloucester attempted it in *King Lear*, and, after the fair Ophelia had thrown herself into the water, Hamlet contemplated it as has no other before or since. Shakespearean suicides resulted from melancholia (the term for depression), the threat of imminent shame and disgrace, or, more frequently, some form of "love's labour lost."

To say the least, all classes of seventeenth-century English society were exposed to a variety of examples and reflections regarding suicide in Shakespeare's plays, except for the period 1642–1660, when Parliament closed the theaters on grounds of their inherent immorality, until the Restoration under Charles II. Like most of the other subjects that were the "stuff" of his plays, suicide was already a part of daily life. As with so many other everyday experiences, the Bard simply lifted the issue to new heights of reflection, as well as to the pinnacle of literary expression.

Because those characters were major, if not always heroic, figures, and died a self-chosen death without prolonged condemnation, viewers of the plays were not "preached to" about the evils and sin of the act. Even when the villain met such a fate, it could be read more as a deserved fate rather than as a crime against the state for not allowing just settlement of a debt. A further dimension comes in the gravediggers' scene, with its clear criticism of the privileges of social class.

The only major work in defense of suicide for some twelve hundred years was written by England's famed cleric and poet, John Donne, Dean of St. Paul's in London 1621–1631. In 1608, during a series of personal crises, he wrote his *Biathanatos* (a combination of Greek words meaning roughly "life-death" or "to die violently," according to Clebsch), in which he argued cogently for suicide as an acceptable act for Christians. Donne based his arguments on three types of law: Nature, Reason, and God as mentioned in chapter 2. His use of Scripture to justify suicide as a Christian act rested primarily on texts from Johannine literature (John 10:11-18; 12:25; 13:37; 15:13; 1 John 3:16), but with references to Exodus 32:32; Job 7:15, 21; Jonah 1:12; 4:3, 9; Matthew 26:39; Romans 9:3; 2 Corinthians 12:15; Galatians 4:15, and Philippians 1:20ff. In his hermeneutics Donne also refuted the arguments of those who had used texts to condemn suicide and showed how direct accounts of the act carried no condemnation from biblical writers.[6]

For all his intense conviction and carefully worked out defense, however, Donne decided not to publish his thoughts. They came to light only in 1647, sixteen years after his death, when the book was published by his son.

The eighteenth century saw the full flowering of the seeds of humanism sown during the Renaissance. Intellectualism focused on a rational approach to all realms of thought and practice, prompting historians to label it the Age of Reason, a description that must not overlook much lingering superstition and belief in magic. Many of the world's most influential writings appeared, and for the first time in centuries suicide was debated openly in philosophic works.

In 1700 a published attack against Donne's *Biathanatos* went so far as to advocate cannibalism rather than starvation, when the option was available.[7] Given that alternative, starvation would be a form of death by choice! In France, Montesquieu and Voltaire argued for suicide, citing both the right of individuals to choose and the insignificance of humans before a cosmic God who would hardly notice if some petty human deserted a post of duty, any more than he would a rat deserting a sinking ship.

Like other aspects of Renaissance thought, philosophical arguments of eighteenth-century writers drew largely upon rational arguments that had been used in classical times. Only occasionally did they refer to biblical texts, but even then, no novel forms of interpretation are to be noted. But in 1790, the Reverend Charles Moore did express a less severe attitude against suicides than that of other clergy before him, particularly in allowing for degrees of condonation in varying circumstances and a lack of condemnation when certainty of motive was absent.

John McManners noted that the number of suicides in England doubled between 1670 and 1706, and doubled again by 1750.[8] Late in the century, another epidemic occurred there, a "scourge" which moved John Wesley, late in his long career and at a time when he was otherwise quite open to new ideas in other areas, to express a most reactionary point of view. In his "Thoughts on Suicide," written in 1790, he lamented the "current madness" sweeping the country and proposed nothing less than public exposure of the bodies as the best remedy.[9]

Wesley did not feel the need to justify his position. He merely assumed that: (1) it was an evil deserving the harshest of measures, and (2) that even though there may have been some psychological reason to excuse such a "madness," the severity of punishment would be justified in order to serve the common good. Whether or not other clerics agreed with his proposed remedy, they seem to have agreed with him in thinking suicide was a universally recognized evil that needed no biblical verification. As in Shakespeare's *Hamlet* in the gravediggers' scene, Wesley was apparently aware of the distinction in current treatment of suicides based on social standing. He affirmed that *all* classes should receive the same severe punishment.

NINETEENTH- AND TWENTIETH-CENTURY INTERPRETATION

Sometime in the 1800s the development of a new approach to the study of human society began. Many of the leaders were French, with scholars from other countries sharing in the discussions. As their ideas advanced, it became clear that a test case was needed to demonstrate to those in other disciplines that there was indeed such a scholarly field as sociology.

It fell upon Émile Durkheim (1858–1917) to write the first clear application of sociological principles. In order to make his case as forcefully as possible, Durkheim chose to show the ways society itself was a contributing factor in the occurrence of suicide. Until his time, the assumption had been that the choice of self-death was solely an individual matter.

The result of Durkheim's book, *Le Suicide* (1897) was two-fold: (1) it clearly demonstrated that sociology was an entirely new field of research and application, and (2) it became a classic in the field of suicidology. While his descriptions, categories, methods, and conclusions have all been challenged, they laid the foundation for a form of social analysis that continues to increase in scope and influence, especially in biblical studies.

As we have seen, when new intellectual ideas take hold, they often affect society's understanding of itself. Because people in society are, by the millions, members of religious communities, the changed self-understandings in one social arena affect self-understandings in the other. One of the reasons suicide is less criticized today is largely due to the realization that it is often brought on by conditions within society as well as by conditions affecting the mind (mental illness) or the soul (sin). This notion lies behind the frequently expressed belief that someone was "driven" to behave in a certain way.

Durkheim, of course, did not draw upon biblical texts in explicating his principles of sociology, although he would have conceded that religious beliefs could, regardless of their ethical content, affect the degree to which one related to society. Thus, a part of society, the church, would be a factor within a sociological study, even though the scientifically oriented studies would not be predicated on the teachings of any one religious group. This is why neither sociology nor suicidology can ignore the history and influence of religious communities, including biblical interpretation, in shaping attitudes and behavior.

This review of the beginnings of sociology is necessary for an understanding of how and why attitudes toward suicide have changed in the twentieth century. The second major influence in attitudinal change lies in the field of psychology. Freud suggested that persons caught within any one of several psychoses or neuroses might commit suicide. This medical insight has not only dominated the fields of psychiatry, psychology, and psychotherapy, it has also provided a way for religious communities to reassess their judgments against that act. The change that came in Roman Catholic canon law in 1983 has been explained in part along the lines of psychological insights. Other religious communities have also been influenced by this field of research. At times, it has seemed that all suicides could be swept under a kind of psychological rug, thus allowing the church to excuse all those who committed the act. That much of society has also responded to this understanding is evidenced in a change in laws. Persons once were automatically arrested for attempting suicide (and in an earlier day sentenced to death for doing so!), but later they were automatically required to undergo psychiatric evaluation.

More recently, however, suicidologists have insisted that there is such a phenomenon as rational suicide, at least to the point where persons otherwise quite functional could, over a long period of time, weigh the pros and cons of such an act, reach a personal decision, make a series of decisions regarding method, place, time, and notification, and then carry out the act according to the well-laid plans.[10]

This recognition of rational suicide is not to lessen professional concern for those acts that are not rational, or for that large group that is ambivalent at the time an attempt is made. It merely notes that we can no longer assume that all suicides are to be explained only in terms of mental illness. The acceptance of this reality will play an increasing role in our ethical wrestling with suicide. (See chapter five.)

What follows is a study of biblical interpretation tracing the different ways Jewish and Christian commentators have treated Saul as a suicide.

SAUL AS A SUICIDE IN THE HISTORY OF EXEGESIS

Earlier references to the accounts of Saul indicate that even within the Bible itself, his story is marked by strong and enigmatic personality traits, differing attitudes toward his accomplishments, and, in spite of obvious wrongdoings, a deep and lingering admiration that affected the lives of many of his followers, especially David and the citizens of Ja'besh-Gil'ead.

It should come as no surprise, then, that twenty-five hundred years of exegesis also reflect a wide spectrum of interpretation. Postbiblical interpreters have dealt with Saul's death in many ways, but a spot check will indicate the major ways in which this primary figure has been viewed as far as his suicide is concerned. Because twentieth-century Jewish interpreters have a special interest in suicide, the history of exegesis within that group deserves to be considered separately. At the same time, such a limited survey falls well within, and contributes to, the purposes of this chapter.

Jewish Interpretation of Saul's Suicide

At one end of the spectrum among Jewish commentators is the outright condemnation of Saul for having committed suicide. He died for his sins, variously identified as disobeying God's commands, sparing Agag of the Amalekites, envy (of David), participation in necromancy, and even robbery. God's punishment, by destroying both his reign and his life, was thus entirely justified.

Others have focused on various legal justifications for his suicide. He was excused because he died for the honor of God and country. Still other rabbis have focused on Saul's death with sympathy. His suicide was necessary in order to maintain the nobility due to a defeated warrior, or the dignity of a royal personage facing a demeaning existence.

Moving a step further, the tractate *Mo'ed Katan* says that God reproached David for celebrating Saul's downfall, and another rabbinic source, *Yebamoth*, states that Saul was not properly mourned. These statements again show that Saul was not remembered for the manner of his death. The *Ta'anith* of the Babylonian Talmud suggests that Saul's death was "imposed" upon him, perhaps seen as a way of removing any blame whatever. *Sanhedrin* 95a transfers the blame to David for having caused the death of Saul, a position directly at odds with the view of Chronicles. *Berekoth* and *'Erubin* affirm that Saul was forgiven because Samuel had promised that Saul would be with him after his death. This point of view stands squarely against the notion that no suicides were ever to receive forgiveness.[11]

Current Jewish interpretations of Saul as a suicide have been strongly influenced by the Nazi-instigated Holocaust of 1933–1945.

The stirring history of Judaism is stained with the blood of numerous mass suicides prompted by severe oppression.[12] The recent work of Yigael Yadin at Masada, and of other archaeologists at Gamla, sites of mass suicides in the first century C.E., have increased the ethical concerns for justifiable suicide. Numerous articles have appeared in the journals *Tradition*, *Judaism*, and *The Reconstructionist*, representing different branches of that faith. Even among these recent discussions, Saul as a suicide is variously interpreted.

In an article entitled "Masada—In the Light of Halakah," Dov I. Frimer of Yeshiva University wrote that the sages clearly understood "some allowances for suicide under specified critical circumstances." He pointed to the account of Saul's death in 1 Samuel based on the king's fear of physical torment as offering what he called "the first working principle" to be used in answering the basic question, "Were the Masada defenders permitted by Torah law to kill themselves?" He then referred to a number of rabbinic interpreters in the Middle Ages who held that "a person who fears . . . unbearable pain is permitted under emergency conditions" to commit suicide.[13]

From this brief survey, three conclusions about Jewish interpretations of Saul as a suicide can be drawn. First, and perhaps most significantly, although some Jewish interpreters condemned Saul for a variety of sins, crimes, and misdemeanors, the Bible itself shows no condemnation whatever for Saul's having taken his own life.

Second, the attitudes toward Saul ran the gamut from unquestioned culpability because of a variety of sins in his lifetime to almost total absolution. These included ultimate forgiveness and eternal rest with Samuel, as well as strong indications that the cause of his downfall and death were due to factors outside himself, perhaps even attributable to the underside of an otherwise all-loving God.

Third, Saul's death continues to be used in different ways by contemporary historians and biblical interpreters in addressing some very serious ethical and religious issues, especially in the lengthening but very real shadow of the Holocaust.

Saul as a Suicide in Recent Christian Thought

In 1953 George B. Caird wrote in *The Interpreter's Bible* that Saul took his life out of fear of what would come when he was captured.[14] He deleted the words that spoke of the Philistines' killing him on the spot, preferring the shorter version that appeared in the Septuagint (a Greek translation of the Hebrew Bible made prior to the Christian era) and in 1 Chronicles 10:6. He considered the Amalekite's story fictitious. Other recent works discounting the authenticity of the account of Saul's death by the hand of another include the *Harper's Bible Dictionary, Oxford Annotated Bible, Jerome Biblical Commentary,* and *Anchor Bible.* But John Mauchline in the *New Century Bible* follows H. P. Smith in the *International Critical Commentary* in accepting the Amalekite's story as genuine. None of these writers gives special attention to the significance of Saul's death as a suicide, an indication that they think the text is not concerned about the subject.[15]

Saul's "melancholia" as the cause of his suicide was mentioned as early as 1922 in the *Encyclopedia of Religion and Ethics.*[16] But the most explicit description of a psychological reason, accepted by many Christians (see the "Exposition" on the text by John C. Shroeder in *The Interpreter's Bible*[17]) was given by Norman Gottwald in *A Light to the Nations*:

> Saul was essentially guileless; in his deepest emotional and mental distress there was a grand integrity about him. In our time we have learned to praise the great qualities of men who were sullied by dark despair and mental agony. . . . Biblical tradition, the synagogue, and the church have been far too niggardly in giving credit to one of the noblest of their progenitors, victim not alone or even primarily of Philistine arms but prey to a demented mind and an ambitious subordinate.[18]

Not only is Saul excused from any crime, as some earlier scholars branded it but he is now lauded for his "grand integrity," done in through no fault of his own, but by an "ambitious subordinate" (we assume David, not the young Amalekite).

One of the newest approaches to biblical interpretation, with implications for an understanding of Saul as a suicide, is the new questioning of traditional understandings of the nature of God. From several quarters, questions have arisen concerning theodicy, the justice of God in the midst of human tragedy. The Jewish Holocaust, the threat of nuclear annihilation, a hermeneutic of suspicion, and some non-traditional theologies have all contributed to the current reassessment.

Among those who suggest to one degree or another that Saul did not deserve the treatment he received by God are J. M. Myers in the *Interpreter's Dictionary of the Bible*, and most emphatically, David M. Gunn in *The Fate of King Saul*.[19]

Gunn goes to some length in comparing Saul to such tragic figures as Macbeth and Othello. Then, he approaches elements of structuralism to ask, "Is struggle against *God* (or 'Fate' [note the title of the book]) in such circumstances positive or negative according to one's own set of values?" Gunn holds that 1 Samuel has "opened up the possibility of viewing Saul as essentially an innocent victim of God, and thus of seeing God in negative as well as positive terms."

While the history of Christian interpretation since the fourth century has reflected pretty much a condemnation of suicide, and at times a bias in its treatment of Saul, there have been, particularly in the twentieth century, significant changes. Historical circumstances today, as in the time of Augustine, Luther, and Donne, still affect interpretation. New theological insights now, as in the time of the apostles or Aquinas, play their part. And new ideas relating to the world and society in the twentieth century, as in the Renaissance and Reformation, bring inevitable questionings of long-held assumptions about what the Bible says. Saul is being viewed differently, which points out once more that attitudinal change is taking place within society and within religious communities.

Before leaving this historical survey of interpretation, two other matters, both relevant for current discussion of suicide, need to be considered.

MARTYRDOM AND SUICIDE

Are those who give their lives for what they believe really suicides? Ask most any group of a dozen or more and you will almost always get three responses—yes, no, and well-it-depends.

Martyrdom, like suicide, is a word everyone seems able to define but disagree on widely once specific cases are discussed. When these two problematic terms are dealt with simultaneously, there is all the more reason to begin with a definition. English dictionaries allow for quite different meanings of martyrdom, including: death accepted, or sought, as punishment or as an inevitable consequence of one's faith; suffering constantly for any reason; and the willing acceptance of discomfort in order to be more highly thought of.[20] It can also be roughly equated with self-sacrifice, in order to provide for others what they would not otherwise receive, or to gain for one's self something considered to be greater than this life, such as a lasting remembrance or eternal salvation.

In the New Testament, the Greek word *martyr* also has different meanings, as good biblical dictionaries point out. Originally, it referred to anyone who professed faith in Christ publicly. Gradually, as such "witnessing" resulted more and more in persecution and death, the word came to mean one who died for the faith. Stephen is often referred to as the first Christian martyr (Acts 7), although he had not had the previous vision or expressed call that was for a time considered necessary for genuine martyrdom.

Over the next three hundred years, almost to the time of Constantine, those who died at the hands of their persecutors because they were Christian, and professed to be so, were considered martyrs. Not all martyrs became saints, and not all saints were martyrs in this sense.

Not infrequently, fanatics would insist on being slain, although Roman officials and local magistrates were quite happy either to ignore the presence of professing Christians or to send them away to end their foolish lives in some other way. Some did so, seeking "martyrdom" by jumping off a cliff. As noted above, one council expunged from the list of saints those who had died by their own hand.

The issues behind the present question thus revolve around two sets of circumstances—motive and opportunity. What was true for early Christianity (and also for late Judaism, although Jewish writers used a term more like "holy ones") remains true in large measure today. People choose to "offer themselves" for many reasons—bearing witness to their religious beliefs, doing their patriotic duty, making life better for their family or friends, or giving their lives on the spur of the moment to save the lives of others. They may also have a more personal reason, perhaps bordering on selfishness—to gain a bit of glory, or to flee an evil or disagreeable world. It was this last reason that prompted many ascetics to become "martyrs" by going into the desert, thus substituting physical punishment and death by persecutors for contemplation and wrestling with Satan and the demons who ravaged the soul.

As for opportunity, the fatal witness was much more available in times of persecution. At other times opportunities had to be created.

Yet, even those who, like Ignatius, sought to make sure they were tortured and put to death, were martyred.

As W. H. C. Frend made clear in his excellent study of *Martyrdom and Persecution in the Early Church*, the church's struggle to resolve the many problems pertaining to martyrdom involved its understanding of a number of theological issues—the nature of God, Christ, humanness, the world, the church, and the end of time.

Biblical writers seldom agreed on any single response to persecution or on the church's relationship to the state. Nor was there agreement by theologians before, or even after Constantine. In that long period of struggle and development, Frend stressed, there was a strong and constant interrelationship involving the wavering positions of the state, diverse and changing attitudes within society, and developing self-understanding of the followers of Christ.

Martyrs are those who, by their own volition, deliberately make the supreme, or at least a major personal sacrifice for a cause they believe in. Conceivably they might die without a chance to witness, or recant, or even to flee. But there must always be some group which is willing to accord them honor for the choice they have made. Ironically, because of persecutions of both Protestants and Roman Catholics in England, each side has its martyrologies and its places of worship dedicated to them where descendants on both sides now worship together. God grant that such will soon be the case in struggles between other Christian and interreligious factions.

As for the relationship between suicide and martyrdom, if one's life is ended by personal choice, in whatever manner or for whatever cause, then, under the definition here used, that death is a suicide, though it may not always have been the intent. Thus many speak of Dr. Martin Luther King, Jr. as a martyr, even though he did not choose to die at the time and place that he did. To put one's life deliberately in a situation where it is known, or expected, that another will take it, is essentially a suicidal act. The final judgment on that act—whether it be considered madness or faithfulness, foolishness or heroism, selfishness or altruism, depends on one's own set of religious, personal, and social values. Most often, the circumstances surrounding such a self-chosen death will also play an important role in that final judgment.

This discussion leads naturally to a second perennial question of particular concern to Christians.

WAS JESUS A SUICIDE?

Origen interprets the Gospel of John as saying that Jesus' death was self-chosen. It remains an open question whether Origen or even the Fourth Evangelist would have used the word for suicide, had it been available. The basic Christian affirmation is that Jesus chose to die on a cross in order to bring salvation to all the world. But problems with such a crass statement about Jesus persist. A common belief is that we should not call Jesus a suicide because he chose the only way he could to remain true to his conviction and to achieve the most worthy of goals. The implication was that the term suicide was too derogatory to be used for Jesus. The *New Catholic Encyclopedia* distinguishes between *direct suicide*, "when one has the intention of causing [one's] own death as a thing desired for its own sake . . . or as a means to an end," and *indirect suicide* "when death itself is not desired, but when it is simply foreseen as a likely consequence of an act."[22]

Yet, from time to time, the opposite view is presented in current literature and drama, as in the Pulitzer Prize-winning play, *'night, Mother*.[23]

The distinction between the human Jesus and the divine Christ, a problem no easier for Christians today than for the gospel writers is given consideration here. The line between the two natures is drawn sharply here. Different pictures the Gospel writers painted of the Passion Story and the ways they formulated their Christologies preclude using this as an easy answer, however. Matthew's Jesus prays in the Garden, "Let this cup pass from me; nevertheless, your will be done." Here is the ever-faithful servant, reluctant to go through death on the cross, but entirely ready to suffer if need be. This is a far cry from the fanaticism that seized so many Christians in succeeding centuries. Neither can this depiction of his death ever be used as an example of a suicide for personal motives.

John's Gospel, in contrast, depicts Jesus as the already risen and now reigning Christ, the one who, even as he walked and ate and talked was always in charge of his own destiny and never at the mercy of human rulers. This Christology is so high that the humanness of Jesus, and his involvement in choosing the cross, is a rather minor concern in that Johannine christological context.

The question must be answered in part by how we define suicide and in part how we view Jesus, the Christ. On the human side, he was ready, though reluctant, to die as a witness to his understanding of God, and for the cause of helping others see God in a new way. On the divine side, there was no real "choice" involved. It was all part of a divine plan. It was Jesus' hour of glory. He knew he could lay down his life, and also take it up again. The human dimension of "choice" is virtually inconsequential, even though Donne and many others before and since have understood John's portrait to stand as an example.

Between these two understandings of Jesus, these two Christ-ologies, the question of whether his death was a suicide must be answered—yes, no, or well-it-depends. One other answer is also possible—all of the above. That is because the nature of Christ, which was of such concern for the church after Constantine, was finally declared to be both human and divine.

To say the least, Christians must still be willing to die for their faith in the One who died for them, whenever it seems God's will that they do so. Though fanaticism is always suspect, allowance must be made for those who would model their lives on the example of Jesus—in witnessing to a faith and even giving their lives for others. This position, however, in no way justifies taking one's own life for any selfish motive.

CONCLUSION

The result of this historical survey is twofold. It reviews a broad range of actual uses of Scripture, and it reminds all those concerned for the Bible and suicide that the interpretation of Scripture, when used for guidance for faith-oriented decisions, is always influenced by the times in which its readers live. The Bible was not written in a vacuum and it is never interpreted in one. This background should be kept in mind whenever we consider the moral issues involved in community and personal response, which is the subject of the final chapter.

5

The Ethics of Suicide

At the beginning of chapter 4 we noted the rather frequent occasions when biblical interpretation is modified in response to social change, in contrast to the far less frequent instances in which society's attitudes and behavior are changed as a result of religious thought and action. Each of these realities may be seen in both the Bible and in the history of religious movements, so that acknowledging these realities today does not constitute an attack upon either the authority of Scripture or tradition. That authority always rests upon a faith commitment, whether it ignores the facts or incorporates them.

For religious communities, awareness of the latter reality, that is, that theology and religious practice can at least occasionally influence society, should be a genuine source of encouragement. Changes *can* be made, today as in the past. Margaret Pabst Battin was writing primarily for those in the medical profession when she expressed the hope of effecting a change in the attitudes of society toward suicide:

> Ideological change may occur as part of the natural evolution of a culture, or such change can be engineered. The contemporary world is already familiar with deliberate attitude and values manipulation, from the gentle impress of advertising to the intensive programming and conditioning associated with various religious and political groups.

If our attitudes and values in other areas can be deliberately changed, it is not at all unreasonable to think that our conceptions of the conditions under which suicide would be the rational choice can be changed too.[1]

Battin, a philosopher, has made significant contributions to the discussion of ethics among suicidologists. Other participants, often through articles in *Suicide and Life-Threatening Behavior*, the official journal of the American Association of Suicidology, have included psychiatrists, sociologists, and nurses. Religious communities can be grateful for these expressions of genuine ethical concern on the part of so many in secular professions. Their contributions do not, however, lessen the responsibility of religious groups themselves to do their own ethical reflection, using all the information and insights they can gain from other sources, particularly those who are most directly involved theoretically and practically in matters related to suicide.

Religious faith is directly, and inevitably, related to the behavior of the believer, and of the community of believers. The most reclusive mystic, by attempting to escape from all worldly affairs, is nevertheless "involved" in what is going on in the surrounding world. As Simeon Stylites sat atop his stone pillar, he was not only seeking to bring himself nearer to heaven, he was also making a social, political, and ethical statement, just as surely as any head of state, though certainly less effectively.[2]

Ethics is that branch of knowledge concerned with how humans make choices on the basis of their values and systems of belief. It is always personal, but by that very fact, it is also social. How one person acts, or fails to act, affects to some extent the whole of society. That insight lay at the heart of Athenian democracy. To be human was to be involved in the affairs of the city, the *polis* (the Greek word which is the root of politics and police). Aristotle summed it up: "Man is by nature a political animal." Making the right choice was always related to a knowledge of facts, a system of values, and the use of reason.

Suicide is unquestionably a social phenomenon, as well as an intensely personal matter. The extent to which social conditions contribute to the occurrence of suicide continues to be debated, but there can be no questioning of the fact that 500,000 individual decisions for self-chosen death each year have an enormous effect on American society.

How religious communities use the Bible to reach ethical decisions about suicide has been central to all that has been presented so far, even when the discussion has focused primarily on individual responses. Were it not for this essential social dimension, the present work would be of quite limited use.

In this concluding chapter attention is directed to suicide as an ethical question confronting religious communities, particularly those within the United States. The four topics in this chapter are designed to help those concerned with ethical questions and decisions to see both the multiplicity of the issues as well as their interrelationships. A clear idea of the breadth and complexity of the problem will alleviate the problem of not knowing where to begin. It is precisely this complexity, and the resulting confusion, uncertainty, and discouragement, along with a lack of understanding of what the Bible says and does not say, that have kept most religious communities from addressing suicide with the urgency and careful attention it deserves in the midst of today's crisis.

Within this larger web of relationships, biblical interpretation plays an important role, and it must be employed very carefully. It simply will not do for a single verse or passage to be "applied" to one type of problem, while another verse or passage is used to resolve a different ethical dilemma. That kind of patchwork approach leads only to frustration or shortsighted responses. I am not offering simple biblical answers to each and every ethical question one might encounter while studying suicide. A. Alvarez put the matter succinctly in the preface to his popular study of the subject, *A Savage God*: "No single theory will untangle an act as ambiguous and with such complex motives as suicide."[3] What I am pointing out are ways in which those committed to the Bible as a major source in determining their ethical behavior might be both better informed and more mature in choosing their response to suicide.

The larger, complex issue needs to be broken down into basic sub-categories where people are actually encountering decisions about suicide. This type of analysis is rarely addressed by Christian ethicists interested in suicide or by suicidologists who have expressed their ethical concerns. What follows in this first section is an effort to help us see our way more clearly as we address specific responses to be made by the church and other religious communities.

Any ethical decision regarding suicide, especially when the biblical evidence has been interpreted in so many diverse ways, must also rely on a theological context. An example of how the two work together is then given. This section also includes my answers to some of the questions raised in the overview of ethical problems.

A third section summarizes the statements recently adopted by three religious bodies within the United States—one Presbyterian, one United Methodist, and one Jewish. These responses, though few in number, are quite encouraging, and we trust they shall lead other religious judicatories to formulate their own directives to be used by their respective members.

In the final section, I suggest specific steps the church, and perhaps other non-Christian religious communities as well, might take to make a faithful and mature response to the current crisis within American society.

FOUR AREAS IN WHICH ETHICAL ISSUES ARISE

The first broad category in which a significant group of ethical questions are clustered comes from within society itself. It is here that the national statistics cited in the introduction are to be used. Suicidologists continue to lament that we are hampered by not having a generally accepted definition of suicide and a more responsible approach to reporting suicides. Even so, the figures available make it clear that the whole of society is affected by the phenomenon and incidence of suicide, and that we, as citizens, must be concerned with ethical questions that are social in origin. Many of these have been listed here, arranged in five sub-categories.

1. One clear example of an ethical problem for society is that of priority. How does suicide rate in urgency when compared with other social concerns such as nuclear disarmament, sexism, racism, and substance abuse? Where should our limited resources of time, personnel, and money be placed? (At present, two federal agencies share responsibility for work in the area of suicide: the Centers for Disease Control and the National Institutes on Mental Health. Other federal agencies have been involved in specific areas of the problem, in addition to those at state and local levels.) Is suicide largely a white, middle-class obsession? Or, does it reach into a far larger segment of society than we are willing to admit? If so, do all

segments of society have equal access to professional services that could aid attempters and survivors?

2. What is the responsibility of the media? Are documentaries, dramas, and their propensity for sensationalism a help or a hindrance? Who should be responsible for finding out – the government, private research institutions, or the media? Who sets the standards? Are journalists wise and sensitive in reporting individual cases? Can they be accused of glamorizing teenage suicides, thereby making the act more appealing to others? How and by whom should appropriate criteria be enforced?

At least one journalist took the time to question the ethics of publishing the picture of a state official in the act of committing suicide. Joseph Laitin of *The Washington Post* noted that other violent moments captured on film have often received high praise, but only if the deaths occurred in far away places among foreigners. Whether or not such pictures should be printed at home, he argued, "calls for a different measuring rod for taste." His conclusion was that the matter had to be dealt with on a case by case basis.[4]

Apart from an obvious ethnic prejudice, Laitin's column may have been a ploy to keep the heat off his editor, but at least it was a forthright effort to raise the ethical dimension of media responsibility in print. That he failed to reach a clearly defined solution only reflects our pervasive ethical uncertainty.

3. In one of his *Christian Century* editorials, Jim Wall raised the question of "technolatry."[5] Do we, as a society, worship our technological achievements to the point of being blind to their tendencies toward tyranny? Are we programmed to implement every device we invent? Do sophisticated systems prolong life, or do they merely prolong dying?

Or, can we acknowledge that with each new medical protocol and procedure, and with each new invention and drug, we may be coming one step nearer to a truly dramatic breakthrough which could enhance the quality of life for generations to come? It is easy to see why questions related to medical technology, and how it is used, are often applied to euthanasia as well as to suicide.

4. Another set of questions arises with respect to how straightforward society, and especially churches, should be in acknowledging suicide as a genuine ethical problem to be wrestled with, rather than trying to dismiss all suicides as the result of a deranged mind. To

be sure, many suicides occur as the result of severe mental and emotional dysfunction, but while sweeping the whole matter under some
kind of psychological rug has enabled many people to "excuse" an otherwise "sinful" deed, that same notion has often kept both society and
church, including its ethicists and biblical interpreters, from addressing
the issue in an objective manner. Can we, with integrity, go on denying
the findings of some suicidologists that most suicides are *not* the result
of mental illness? Failure to see things as they are certainly prevents
us from addressing the matter in the most responsible manner.

5. Also from the social arena is the question of why three times
as many women attempt suicide as men. Is this statistic related in
any way to blatant sexism? Are we justified in dismissing this startl-
ing ratio on the grounds that women are just naturally more emotional and prone to fake a suicide only to get sympathy?

While most suicides can be described as "cries for help" (by both
men and women!), there are other reasons for this wide discrepancy
between the sexes. A study of one hundred English battered women
showed that fifty of them had attempted suicide while living with
their spouses or lovers. On April 15, 1989, *The Times* of London
cited a Home Office report, which revealed "horrific levels of wife-
beating in Britain," a common social problem affecting all strata of
society. Much of the problem, including the reluctance of officials
to take action against violent husbands and boyfriends, was caused
by assumptions and attitudes regarding men's and women's roles in
society.[6] Has the church helped to create attitudes of male
dominance that foster such violence?

Similar ethical questions growing out of our involvement in society relate to members of ethic minority groups, lesbians and gays,
victims of AIDS, and those with handicapping conditions. Males (aged
20–59) with AIDS are sixty-six times more likely to commit suicide
than the general population, according to a March 1988 report in
the *Journal of the American Medical Association*.

A second broad area in which ethical questions cluster is that
of legislation. Certainly laws have changed. The bodies of suicides
are no longer exposed and desecrated. Survivors are no longer denied their inheritance, even though many still suffer from a cruel
and needless stigma. Suicide has now been decriminalized, but
some states still have laws against attempted suicide and assisted
suicide. These legal conditions are the source of ethical questions.

1. What do we do with laws that are no longer enforced? Do they call for removal, or at least revision? To do so takes legislatures' time and taxpayers' money. Yet, most would agree that it is not desirable for a state or nation to have laws that go uninforced.

Betty Rollin, newswoman for NBC-TV, wrote *Mother's Last Wish*, in which she detailed her decision to help her mother take a lethal dose of pills, and her own role in assisting her suffering parent.[7] Yet, she was interviewed on television in her home state where to assist someone to take their own life is a felony.

2. One of my former students in New Testament Greek was a thoracic surgeon who made a mid-career change and decided to enter the ordained ministry. She paid most of her way through seminary by being in charge of emergency rooms in area hospitals during late hours and weekends.

It was she who pointed out a dilemma people in emergency rooms often face when attempted suicides come in. Must those admitted be sent to a mental hospital for observation? Can they be rational and competent by the time they are brought in? This kind of question points up the relationship between a social problem and a legal one, when society passes laws based on the assumption that all who attempt suicide are mentally unbalanced.

3. Again, if all assisted suicides are wrong, to what extent can we condone the action of the armed forces and the CIA in providing lethal pills for those who enter dangerous situations in which they might be captured and tortured by the enemy? Both Gary Powers, the U2 pilot who made illegal reconnaissance flights over Russia before his capture, and Oliver North, key figure in the Iran-Contra hearings, have said publicly that their superiors made such offers to them. Public reports have been made that the FBI once wrote to Dr. Martin Luther King, Jr., urging him to take his own life.[8]

4. The legal dilemmas have also surfaced in relationship to medical technology. Does a person have a right to refuse therapy and forced feeding?

5. Another legal problem is posed by the easy access to handguns. If more than half of all suicides are committed by firearms, does society have a moral obligation to control access to such weapons, apart from their frequent use in robberies, rapes, and accidental deaths? The state of Maryland passed a law in 1988 prohibiting the sale and ownership of handguns, over strenuous efforts to defeat it by the National Rifle footrAssociation.

The ready accessibility of dangerous weapons has been cited as a contributing factor in the high rate of suicide among police officers, which is sometimes 500 to 600 percent above the national average. This statistic was reported on the NBC evening news for February 2, 1987. The leading cause was given as the stress of police duty. This problem is not limited to the United States. *Talking Blues* is a 1989 work by Robert Graef, author and film director, summarizing attitudes of British police officers in their own words.[9] He noted that the Royal Ulster Constabulary in Northern Ireland suffers from an exceptionally high incidence of alcoholism and suicide. Spouses of officers have also been known to use government-issued weapons for self-destruction.

6. To mention one more legal problem, the large number of suicides in our jails and prisons should be noted. What is the proper role of officers, wardens, and other administrators, as well as the state, in providing proper care for inmates? To what extent should officials be prosecuted by survivors for not ensuring physical safety for those placed in their care? As mentioned in the introduction, there have been recent lawsuits in which families of victims won their cases, claiming neglect in proper care.

A third broad area where ethical questions arise is in the arena of politics.

1. The most obvious examples here are the deaths of those motivated by a cause. How do we view such deaths? Not only Buddhist monks in Vietnam but also one American Quaker at the Pentagon immolated himself in protest against that conflict. Not only did Mahatma Gandhi fast to the point of death for the oppressed millions in India, but Mitch Snyder lost the sight of one eye, later restored, fasting for the thousands of homeless in the nation's capital.

Multiply the individuals. Multiply the causes. From Colin P. Kelly and the Japanese kamikaze pilots in World War II, to IRA leaders who starved themselves to death in prisons, to Iranian fanatics who led willing children across enemy-laid mine fields, millions are affected by the outcome of suicide. Are we to condemn all of them, or do we once again go on a case by case basis, depending on whether or not we agree with the cause being advocated?

2. Governor Toney Ayana commuted the death sentences of five convicts — a legal and social matter — on the basis of personal religious convictions. But, as with any politician, an official act is immediately

evaluated in terms of the voters, whether or not the political repercussion was a central concern in the beginning. People who hold that only God has the right to take a life seldom show concern for the matter of their right to prolong life, even when the person involved may not want it. Traditionally, the reason has been that because God gave life, we are to prolong it. These and other moral dilemmas require careful thought, lest in applying faith to practice our method becomes too slipshod and irresponsible.

3. In the broad concern for politics and Christian ethics, the conviction of Dietrich Bonhoeffer in his attempt to assassinate Adolph Hitler has been admired. His theology and ethics are still studied and quoted. He is deeply revered for his keen insights and profound thought, deep Christian conviction, and final martyrdom just days before he would have been liberated from prison.

Yet, his own position on suicide was clearly in line with the teachings of Augustine. In his *Ethics* Bonhoeffer said,

> God has reserved to himself the right to determine the end of life, because he alone knows the goal to which it is his will to lead it. . . . Even if his earthly life has become a torment for him, he must commit it intact into God's hand, from which it came.[10]

So, not everyone with a political cause is driven to choose suicide as a form of witness, and some would not condone it under any circumstance. At the same time, even Bonhoeffer made his famous decision to join the murder plot knowing full well that it might lead to his death, and he no doubt would have gone on with it even if he had known in advance that he would die as a result. In the Roman Catholic tradition, there is the notion of a second intent. The first, on which Bonhoeffer is to be judged, was to bring peace and freedom to others. The second, his own death, was only a possible consequence of the initial "moral" decision.

A fourth area of society in which ethical problems arise relates to pastoral care. Not all citizens are directly involved here, but similar questions frequently confront doctors, nurses, social workers, and non-religious counselors, as well as friends.

1. The phone rings late at night. You answer it and hear, "Pastor, is it a sin to commit suicide?" You know the voice. You know the troubled, depressed spirit behind it. And so you answer, "Yes, it *is!*"

In this case, the "you" is a sensitive, exceptionally intelligent young woman pastor with several years of very effective ministry in the parish. There was no question in her mind that she had given the only answer she could at that moment, which allowed her time to render further pastoral counseling and make the proper referral. But is this approach justified in every case? Can we make it standard practice to falsify our beliefs in the hope of bringing about a result we are convinced is better for the individual and others as well?

2. For centuries, the church has distorted much of the biblical evidence to support a position it had reached primarily on non-biblical grounds. Have we been totally honest in this regard, or have we compromised our biblical integrity for a supposedly higher moral cause? To what extent does our preferred eisegesis keep us from the more rigorous and often more threatening demands of serious exegesis?

3. Those involved in pastoral care, as well as those who work in the field of suicidology, have expressed deep concern over the stigma attached to the attempters and the survivors. At a 1987 national conference on Youth Suicide Prevention attended by some four hundred professionals, several references were made by the speakers to this unfortunate reality in society. Given fifteen hundred years of Christian teaching, the cause of that stigma in society lies directly at the doorstep of the church. Now we face the question: Is such stigma, so long used to prevent suicide, only another barrier to overcome in the prevention of that same act? For many in the field, the answer is a clear yes. Should religious communities now work to remove the stigma their foreparents helped to create? If so, how might they go about doing so?

4. Yet another tough question for pastors, and for an increasing number of laity as well: To what extent would you affirm, or share in, a family decision to honor the plea of a suffering loved one to end all dramatic means of life-support or even to take their own life more directly? How would you counsel a group of friends who came wanting to know how to respond to such a plea? If you supported the decision, would you, if asked, be present when the plug was pulled, or the pills taken?[11]

Most writers on the subject say that such a decision should be made by the patient, family, and friends. By sharing the responsibility, there is less likelihood that the patient would make a hasty choice before considering all the options. The support group would also be better able to deal with the psychological, or perhaps legal results that might follow.

5. In terms of serious study, if not advocacy, would we encourage our religious community to invite a representative of the Hemlock Society to talk about the "best," that is, the least violent, painful, messy, bothersome, and most certain ways of committing suicide? There are now more than twenty organizations in some seventeen countries which openly provide information like this. Should such a book ever be part of a church library?

These are indeed tough questions. Some would argue that they should not even be asked. I have deliberately stated them in order to show as clearly as possible the serious, painful, far-reaching, yet intensely personal dimensions of the ethical issues raised by suicide. Only by facing them honestly and forthrightly can religious communities make a mature, faithful response. In the next section, I present one biblical/theological context out of which answers to such questions might come.

CONFRONTING SUICIDE
FROM A PERSONAL PERSPECTIVE

An overall statement on the ethics of suicide, based on "what the Bible says" on the subject, is in order. By putting the phrase in quotes, I am of course suggesting that whatever use one might make of the Bible for ethical decisions needs to be determined with a number of factors in mind. These I have referred to in the preceding pages. What follows is my own approach to relating Christian faith and biblical understandings of God and humanity to the specific issue of suicide. One issue deeply affects both individuals and the society in which we live, and so, necessarily it is one that the church must address. To understand the biblical/theological context out of which I approach the subject and make the decisions given, consider the basic elements in that web of relationships.

THE AUTHORITY OF THE BIBLE

The Bible is the only source Christians have for the life of Jesus, their Savior, and the beginnings of the church. Those accounts themselves were first remembered, related, and recorded by persons whose lives had been transformed by their experience and their belief that the God known among the Jews had, in the Christ event, come to them in a new way.

Their interpretation of that event, whether in oral or written form, was at every point affected by the peculiar forces at work within their society and the religious community in which they lived, as well as by their own unique understanding of the events which had transpired among them. In that respect they were at one with the biblical writers who had preceded them. A study of the Hebrew Bible shows the many ways in which its writers were affected by their times as they perceived and responded to the activity of God in the world, in politics, and in their personal lives.

It was that response of faith, and particularly the way biblical writers called for a certain behavior within their religious communities, that constituted the core of ethical teachings for Jews and Christians. At times, the commands were quite simple and direct. At others, they were not so simple and far less direct. Not infrequently, new questions arose on old issues. Occasionally, later biblical writers reworked earlier texts, giving them an interpretation that made more sense and gave more help to their own times and circumstances. Ever since, many ethical and legal decisions have had to be rethought in the light of new circumstances and of new understandings of both God and humanity.

To acknowledge these facts in no way requires a lessening of one's credence in the authority of the Bible as sacred Scripture. To say the least, it can be seen simply as the way God inspired the writers to make faith applicable to the spiritual and often practical needs of their day. Our task is always to ask first, what were those inspired writers actually saying (or not saying) to their people. Only then can we ask how that biblical understanding can best aid us today.

BELIEFS ABOUT GOD AND HUMAN BEINGS

For religious persons, what is believed about the nature of God and of human beings is as basic to making ethical choices as a knowledge of the method chosen to interpret Scripture. Although we would all prefer to think our beliefs about theology and anthropology are "biblical," the fact is that different views of each are affirmed in different parts of the Hebrew and Christian Scriptures. In short, an ethical decision made without some clarity on these two subjects is not as "biblical" as it should be.

My own biblical/theological context begins by affirming God as the ultimate giver of life. Even our parents are not entitled to sole credit for our existence, however "planned" their parenthood might have been. The biblical basis for this theological statement begins with the creation stories and is reaffirmed throughout the rest of the Scriptures.

It is this affirmation that prevents my credit, or allegiance, to any other source for my existence. Thus, God is also, as I read the Bible, the One whose unconditional claim is at the same time the source of freedom for all humanity. Such freedom confers also a dignity upon all persons, one which is not subject to any human criterion. So seeing God as creator of life and bestower of freedom upon all humanity relates theology to anthropology, the nature of God to the nature of human beings.

In the constant reevaluation and reformulation of my own theological context, based in no small measure on what I learn from the praxis of faith in community and the world, I return again and again to those troublesome, even dangerous words of Paul to the Galatians: "For freedom Christ has set us free" (Gal. 5:1). Simply, perhaps too simply put, the reason for Christ's coming was nothing other than to enable us to be truly free, no strings attached. Here of course, my Christology is an intimate part of my theology and my anthropology.

A SYSTEM OF ETHICS

Developing a system of ethics moves us another step toward the goal of practical decision making. From the interpretation of Scripture (including an awareness of the hermeneutical method being used) and a formulation of our understanding of the nature of God and humanity, and usually of Christ, the "how" of our ethical task must also be considered. What guidelines should be followed—medical knowledge, the law, "common sense," tradition, what "feels" right? What priorities will be established—what's best for all, the rights of the individual, national duty? What method could be used in putting it all together?

My conviction is that the freedom God has given to all human beings at the moment of creation, with its consequent dignity for each individual, is to be maintained, encouraged, and supported in every way possible. This means, on the one hand, allowing wide latitude in individual choices, but at the same time, making sure that personal behavior does not diminish the dignity or freedom of others. Not to respect and defend these gifts from God is to deny our own dignity and to relinquish our own freedom ("to submit again to the yoke of slavery" as Paul said) and it is to fail to acknowledge the source of those divine gifts. In a word, it is idolatry in its most tragic form.

These then are the guidelines, the priorities, and the method of putting it all together. The next step is to make some decisions about the ethical problems raised in the preceding section.

CONCLUSIONS

Among the numerous, interrelated questions that arise when suicide is considered as an ethical issue, some seem more urgent, and are more frequently asked than others. While all deserve attention by religious communities seeking to be fully responsible, I address now those which seem to be the most pressing and which illustrate a reliance upon the biblical/theological context just discussed.

Two issues affecting the whole of society need immediate attention by religious communities. First, the persistent myths about suicide—talking about it only causes it, those who say they are going to never will, a strong stigma is the best prevention, only the mentally ill take their own lives—these need to be overcome. Each of these is now seen as a barrier to prevention. Stigma still exists, though not in the extreme form of the past, and is clearly contrary to the freedom and dignity discussed above. Because the church has both fostered and followed myths like these, there is a special reason for its members to repent of the errors of the past.

The second urgent matter in the whole of society concerns the attitudes toward women and men. Belief in the right of men to dominate, as studies continue to show, is often a major cause of battering to their wives and lovers and of rape among strangers, and even within families. No wonder suicide is exceptionally high among their victims, including abused children. Religious teachings again must share the blame for society's unjust attitudes, legislation, and lack of equity in treatment by police and courts in such matters. As long as these conditions exist, all talk of freedom and dignity has a hollow and horrible ring.

In the area of legislation, society is not aided by having bad laws on the books, but experience has shown that attempting to remove them often diverts money and energy from more urgent needs in that same field. It should best fall to legislators, lawyers, and judicial leaders to make their own studies of these issues, perhaps at the urging of religious communities. To leave outdated laws until a specific case arises may well result in injustice.

With extreme care and in clearly defined cases of terminal illness, a way needs to be found for individuals and the close circle of caring friends and family, to have more freedom in making a decision regarding a self-chosen death, so long as the dignity, wishes, and rights of the individual are preserved. In cases where these conditions were met, the information on the "best" method, as one might find in publications of The Hemlock Society, should be available, and, if possible, the services of a responsible physician. No legal action should then be involved.

Related to legislation is the dire matter of suicides in jails and prisons. Those in charge of arrested offenders have a special responsibility to see that all persons in their care are protected from self-destruction. This, too, falls under the broad, though somewhat ironic heading of freedom and dignity.

Politics and religion have a long mutual history indeed, as biblical writings and a study of the church and Judaism make abundantly clear. In many instances today, they still come together in a most grim way as people choose to die, often dramatically, for one cause or another out of religious conviction. The decision as to who is a martyr and who is not will always be made on the basis of a particular set of values that are affected by the mesh of religious ideals and political realities.

Given the emphasis on freedom and dignity, as well as countless examples from Bible and tradition, it seems the better part of wisdom and charity to rely heavily on God's mercy for those who choose to die on behalf of others in this way. At the same time, those who survive are called to reexamine most carefully their own beliefs, teachings, and actions, lest such examples become all too common, destroying the freedom of others.

I trust my own decisions on these matters will indicate how the Bible, a method of biblical interpretation, and a theological context might be used in confronting ethical issues in suicide today. More important than what I believe, however, is the need for religious communities and individuals to reflect seriously upon their own biblical and religious understandings, make their own decisions, and move to meet some of the urgent needs within society and their own faith groups.

THREE STATEMENTS ON SUICIDE
BY RELIGIOUS COMMUNITIES

It continues to be a source of discouragement that so few religious groups have set forth any official position on suicide. Inquiries to more than a dozen national offices have resulted in only the three that are reviewed here. On the encouraging side, however, is that all of these have been formulated in recent years, which may presage a wider response. Also on the positive side is the growing number of churches and synagogues that are becoming involved in suicide prevention, intervention, and postvention across the United States.

This section reviews the three statements in order to show the way religious communities are beginning to respond officially in terms of biblical, ethical, and pastoral perspectives.

1. In 1972 the General Assembly ôf The Presbyterian Church in the United States created its Council on Theology and Culture, which, among other duties, was empowered to conduct studies on social issues and to make reports and recommendations to the parent body. Topics have included subjects from abortion to liberation theology. In 1981 the General Assembly adopted a lengthy paper on "The Nature and Value of Human Life," which gave attention to several life-threatening situations. Two pages addressed suicide, and eight were a study guide to assist local congregations in presenting the issues.[12]

Those who wrote the document duly recognized the "range of possible actions" that could fall under the definition of suicide and noted that morally, all actions should not be considered alike. They separated the acts of 1) sacrificing oneself; 2) allowing oneself to die; and 3) taking one's own life. The paper stated that sacrificing oneself for another (whether in combat or in peacetime) is morally commendable but not morally obligatory.

In cases where dying persons can make a rational decision not to survive on treatments that prolong dying, there is no condemnation if persons refuse such medical aid. Death here is not in itself a harm. Basic to this argument, and the argument for enforcing life-sustaining treatment, are the twin obligations to do no harm and to protect life.

The third possibility, taking one's own life, comes closest to the traditional definition of suicide, which tradition has most blatantly condemned. Even here, the language is cautious: no outright condemnations, only the recognition that some suicides are not likely to be justified.

Other comments noted the ambiguities that surround many suicides, thus lessening any need for condemnation; the need for compassionate counsel and support for attempters and survivors, and the imperative to correct social conditions that foster suicidal tendencies. The final statement reflects the shift in attitude already noted: "Whatever our judgment about the morality of actions in this sphere, we need to take care never to call into question the abounding love of God for those prompted to such anguished acts of self-destruction."[13]

One has but to compare the Shorter Catechism, a basic document for most Presbyterians, to see what a significant shift has taken place:

Q. 68. What is required in the [You Shall Not Kill] commandment?
A. [This] commandment requireth all lawful endeavors to preserve our own life and the life of others.   ˙
Q. 69. What is forbidden in this commandment?
A. [This] commandment forbiddeth the taking away of our own life, or the life of our neighbor unjustly, or whatsoever tendeth thereunto.[14]

2. The official policy-making body of The United Methodist Church is its General Conference. At its quadrennial meetings the denomination's boards, agencies, or even individual members, present resolutions to be adopted as directives and guidelines for the entire church for the next four years, or until such time as the resolutions might be changed. In 1988 the General Conference approved, for the first time, a resolution on suicide.

The five-page statement grew out of a working conference on suicide held in 1987. Twenty-five leaders from across the church heard and discussed papers on biblical, psychological, social, and ethical perspectives. After approving a first draft while still in session the participants responded to two later revisions by mail before the document was unanimously approved by the denomination's Board of Church and Society. After further study and discussion by the General Conference, two changes were made before the resolution was adopted: a sentence was deleted because it could have been construed as approving suicide under less than unusual cases, and several statements recommending courses of action by various boards and agencies were changed to specific directives to do so. That is, the *should's* were changed to *will's!*

Without benefit of the earlier Presbyterian statement, the United Methodists began pretty much where that document ended, opening with Paul's bold affirmation of faith in Romans 8:38-39 that nothing can separate us from the love of God. After noting that well-intentioned Christians in the past had "often contradicted Christ's call to compassion," the resolution set forth its purpose: "to encourage the sharing of God's grace in circumstances involving suicide and to offer a word of faith and hope to all who are affected by the tragedy of suicide."[15]

Informative segments on demographics and causes preceded the guidelines and directives for the denomination. Among the specifics: major initiatives to prevent suicide; priority attention to survivors, including the denunciation and abandonment of harsh and punitive measures (such as the refusal to permit funeral rites inside the church); efforts to change social attitudes toward suicide; provision for adequate pastoral care; and, elimination of social conditions and public policies that devalue human life.

Once again, we can see how far many of today's Methodists have come from the view of their founder, John Wesley, who would have had the bodies of all suicides exposed as a means of prevention.

3. The third official statement on suicide by a religious body was drawn up and circulated by the Task Force on Youth Suicide for the Union of American Hebrew Congregations.[16] Entitled "The Value of Life: (The Reform Jewish View of Suicide)," and prepared by Rabbis Bernard Zlotowitz and Ramie Arian, the one-page statement began: "Reform Judaism does not condone the taking of one's life." But a sign of the times is reflected in the second sentence: "Suicides are automatically considered as not having been capable of understanding their own actions (*lo la-da-at*)."

As a result of this *non compos mentis* assumption, they urge counseling for attempters who survive and the conducting of rites to those succeeding in taking their own lives.

A second paragraph sets forth the basic position of Orthodox Judaism (explicitly rejected by Reform Judaism) that the soul of a suicide goes to Hell (*gehenom*) and no funeral rites are permitted. Burials are to be made only on the periphery of the cemetery and away from other grave sites. But, if the suicide is judged to have been mentally incompetent, then such restrictions do not apply.

The statement concludes with a paragraph noting the current epidemic of suicide among youth and affirms that the Union of American Hebrew Congregations will respond by teaching and emphasizing "the value and holiness of life as a God-given gift to be held in sacred trust." One's own life is unique and has special meaning to others. Thus, in traditional language, "The saving of one life — including his or her own life — is tantamount to saving the world."

Although quite limited in scope, this document shows the impact made by current statistics and modern psychology, while at the same time responding in a charitable way with an emphasis on the positive values of life. Because values continue to play an essential role for any religious community as it addresses a major social issue, they must be clearly understood as the issue is studied and as ethical decisions are made.

Those who work through the questions, facts, and perspectives presented in these official statements will be better informed in a number of areas and will have a better chance of seeing both the breadth and complexity of suicide more clearly. From that improved vantage point, they can move toward a more rational and mature response to the continuing tragedy of our day. Central to all ethical deliberation is the question, How can we be open to a more humane, compassionate response without giving the impression that suicide is acceptable for anyone under any circumstance?

WHAT RELIGIOUS COMMUNITIES CAN DO

Following a *Christian Century* article in which I pointed out the church's failure to deal with the current crisis, I was criticized for not having given answers to the questions I had raised.[17] The point was well taken, even though the purpose of the article was to serve as a kind of theological and ethical gadfly to get others to go about answering the questions for themselves.

My own response to that specific criticism was first to ask specific ethicists, preachers, and denominational leaders to join me in moving the church. Secondly, I responded by formulating my own thoughts as to what the church and other religious communities could be doing.

It is a source of some comfort to know that at least two leaders in Christian ethics and one in sociology have written on the subject as a result of my nagging, that a few pastors have decided to preach on it, and that several churches and C.P.E. groups have conducted classes and seminars on various aspects of the problem. I have edited two books, one on sermons and the other on various perspectives, each designed to help religious groups to make a more faithful response. In addition, I helped to initiate and guide the resolution adopted by the United Methodist General Conference. I can only hope that these results will indicate what can be done by religious groups and individuals, and that the overall response will help to bring about a reduction in the number of suicides and a more humane, caring environment for all those in need.

It remains now only to present a few suggestions as to what churches, and perhaps other religious groups, might do to respond to the current crisis. These thoughts are based in part on an article I wrote for *Response*, a publication for United Methodist Women, in October, 1986.[18] At that time, I identified some specific programs that could be implemented immediately to begin moving the church.

1. Each of us can be more pastoral. Human compassion to those who are in pain and in need of help is so thoroughly grounded in the Bible that it calls for little or no comment. When the tragedy of suicide occurs, or is imminent, we can do everything possible to comfort and strengthen the suffering and bereaved. Suicidologists insist that the removal of the age-old stigma will be a positive contribution to the prevention of suicide.

2. We can be better informed, especially on ways of identifying suicidal behavior and knowing when to intervene. Teenagers especially need to learn to recognize when their peers are giving the slightest hint of suicidal behavior, and to realize that they must take such signals seriously. They must also be able to intervene effectively. We can all learn which of the many agencies are ready to provide proper help, and we can help publicize those resources.

3. We can do our biblical and theological homework. While pastors carry the major responsibility for leading congregations to engage in Bible studies and helping them to do their theological task, lay persons can make sure that such needs and opportunities are not overlooked. It would not be improper to ask, When did we last hear (preach) a sermon on suicide, other than at a funeral?

4. We can work for better understanding in our communities. Unfortunately, there are some Christians who are still quite ruthless in their responses to the bereaved. There are also many who, fearing recrimination, do not feel free to tell their story, and so continue to carry the burden of unresolved grief, guilt, anger, and resentment. Some churches are beginning to take an active role in providing opportunities for those with such needs to meet together for mutual support.

Archaic laws need to be taken off the books if no one really believes them to be just, or if they are being ignored. Concerned citizens can establish local crisis centers, and they can urge public officials to assume leadership in getting the job done. Still others can work to lessen the number of suicides in jails and prisons.

5. We can urge our own denomination or judicatory to clarify its position, to publicize it, and to urge its study and implementation.

6. We can proclaim the gospel! Strange as it may seem, the good news of that grace which makes each life precious and free can be the basis for helping the helpless and giving hope to the hopeless. Evangelism, in the best sense of sharing the good news, as well as the abundant life, can be a source of liberation that gives rich or poor, young or old, of whatever class or color, a sense of belonging and meaning in life that can offset many of the reasons why people commit suicide. Shalom is that concept from Hebrew Scriptures which seeks holistic well-being for each member of the community. It is a concept that would be particularly helpful for congregations that take seriously their obligation to love each of their neighbors and all the members of their neighborhood.

To these I would add yet another, as expressed in some of the denominational statements cited above: we can work within social structures to eliminate those dehumanizing economic, educational, medical, and prison conditions and all prejudices against minorities that contribute to despair, a sense of worthlessness, and a lack of hope among our fellow citizens. In all things, we are to love each other as God has loved us.

In times of unparalleled tragedy such as we are facing in America today, religious communities should not be in the background. Our concern, our thought, our energies, and our faith are desperately needed to help turn the tide. Fortunately, there are things we can do.

Notes

PREFACE

1. Lucy Davidson, "Psychological Perspectives," *Perspectives on Suicide*, edited by James T. Clemons (Louisville: Westminster/John Knox Press, 1990). In a lecture given in 1987, Davidson noted that some coroners estimate the number of suicides could be 50 percent higher than those actually reported.

INTRODUCTION

1. Figures are from the National Center for Health Statistics, cited in *The Daily Times*, Salisbury, Md., Thursday, October 18, 1984, 7.

2. Butler was interviewed by *U.S. News and World Report*, July 2, 1982, 51–52.

3. "How Can We Help Ourselves Age With Dignity?" *Parade Magazine*, Sunday, May 29, 1988, 4–7.

4. *Duke: A Magazine for Alumni and Friends*, November–December, 1986, 49.

5. Estimates on the number of attempted suicides by youth vary widely, largely because of inaccurate reports on which to base statistics. This estimate was given by Dr. Lucy Davidson, a consultant on suicide to the U.S. Centers for Disease Control. Others run even higher.

6. Davidson, "Psychological Perspectives, 12," and the U.S. Department of Health and Human Services, National Center for Health Statistics, *Monthly Vital Statistics Report*, vol. 38, no. 5, Supplement, September 26, 1989.

7. *The Keene Sentinel* (N.H.), March 6, 1986, 1, 11. The report, which appeared in a "special article" in the *New England Journal of Medicine* 314, No. 10, on (March 6, 1986): 620–24 was entitled "Delayed Effects of the Military Draft on Mortality."

8. *The Washington Post*, Sunday, August 6, 1986, C1–2.

9. Examples of such reports and programs are: "Will They Be With Us Tomorrow?: Chaplains in Suicide Prevention," prepared by the Chaplain Resource Board, A.S. Kirk, [n.d.]; "USAREUR Active Duty Suicides CY 1985," prepared by the U.S. Army Medical Research Unit Europe, Edwin W. Van Vranken, Charles M. McCraig, and Evelyn H. Golembe, 20 June 1986; and Charles P. McDowell and Audrey M. Wright, "Suicide Among Active Duty USAF Members 1981–1986: A Six-Year Analysis," Bolling Air Force Base, August, 1987. See also A. Morgan Parker, *Suicide Among Young Adults* (New York: Exposition Press, 1974), which focuses on suicides among military personnel.

10. Reported by the Associated Press. See *The Washington Post*, Saturday, January 21, 1989, A4.

11. Edwin Shneidman, *Definition of Suicide* (New York: John Wiley and Sons, 1985), 33.

12. "Navajo-Hopi Dispute," *The Christian Century*, August 27–September 3, 1986, 736–37.

13. *The Los Angeles Times*, Saturday, October 19, 1985, 1, 3. See also, "The Vulnerability of Young Japanese Women and Suicide" by Mamoru Iga, Joe Yamamoto, and Thomas Noguchi, *Suicide*, Vol 5(4), Winter, 1975, 207–22.

14. *Time Magazine*, August 11, 1986, 29. *The Los Angeles Times* reported the suicide of seventeen-year-old Csilla Molnar, the reigning Miss Hungary, who complained of harassment after winning her crown the year before, July 13, 1986.

15. *The Washington Post*, February 18, 1986, A1, 18.

16. Richard Cohen, "Critic at Large," *The Washington Post Magazine*, October 25, 1987, 9.

17. *The Toledo Blade*, Saturday, December 24, 1988, 3.

18. "Suicide: The Silent Signals," produced by Instructional Video Productions, Inc., in cooperation with the National Sheriffs' Association and the Sheriff's Office of Suffolk County, New York. The cassette and a study guide are available from the National Sheriffs' Association, 1450 Duke Street, Alexandria, VA 22314. The American Association of Suicidology has published several studies on suicides and suicidal behavior among offenders in its official journal, *Suicide and Life-Threatening Behavior*. See, for example, Stuart Palmer and John A. Humphrey, "Offender-Victim Relationships in Criminal Homicide Followed by Offender's Suicide, North Carolina, 1972–1977," vol. 10 (1980), 106–18, and Michael Flaherty, "The National Incidence of Juvenile Suicides in Adult Jails and Juvenile Detention Centers," vol. 13 (1983), 85–94. Margaret Engel reported that eight youths had attempted suicide in less than five months at the District of Columbia Receiving Home for Children, a temporary holding facility for youths awaiting trial or sentencing. See *The Washington Post*, May 30, 1986, A1, 23.

19. Henlee H. Barnette, *Exploring Medical Ethics* (Macon, Ga. Mercer University Press, 1982), 112.

20. These statistics were cited in a letter by Herman J. Kregel, former director of the Berkeley Center for Alcohol Studies, Pacific School of Religion, dated August 23, 1984.

21. James F. Childress, *Priorities in Biomedical Ethics* (Philadelphia: Westminster Press, 1981), 91–92.

22. The National Headquarters address is P.O. Box 27605, Washington, DC, 20038. Membership in 1988 was officially about 1000, with some 200 chapters across the United States.

23. See Paul Gibson, "Gay Male and Lesbian Youth Suicide," in *Report of the Secretary's Task Force on Youth Suicide*, published by the Alcohol, Drug Abuse, and Mental Health Administration, vol. 3, *Prevention and Intervention in Youth Suicide*, DHHS Pub. No. (ADM) 89-1623, Washington, D.C.: Supt. of Docs., U.S. Gov't Print. Off., 1989, 110–37.

24. *The New York Times*, August 16, 1986, A10.

25. *The Baltimore Sun*, Saturday, October 24, 1987, 10A.

26. For one effort to help preachers overcome the reluctance to preach on suicide see *Sermons on Suicide*, edited by James T. Clemons (Louisville: Westminster/John Knox Press), 1989.

27. *People Weekly*, February 10, 1986, 107–9.

28. Émile Durkheim, *Suicide: A Study in Sociology*, translated by John A. Spaulding and George Simpson (New York: Free Press, 1951).

29. Shneidman, *Definitions of Suicide*, vi.

30. Ibid., 5.

31. Ibid., 203.

32. *Suicide and the Right to Die*, edited by Jacques Pohier and Dietmar Mieth, English language editor, Marcus Lefébur (T and T Clark, 1985).

33. Ibid., 63.

34. Ibid., 103.

35. Ibid., 205.

36. Ibid., 206.

CHAPTER 1

1. Elie Wiesel, *Five Biblical Portraits* (Notre Dame, Ind.: University of Notre Dame Press, 1981). So too Margaret Pabst Battin, *Ethical Issues in Suicide* (Englewood Cliffs, N.J.: Prentice Hall, 1982), 29. She does, however, put Jonah in the same "borderline" category.

2. One final text from Genesis must also be mentioned, although it is beyond the scope of our concern. In the account of the destruction of Sodom (Gen. 19:15-28), Lot is told to flee with his family and not look back "lest you be consumed" (v. 17). But his wife disobeys and is turned to a pillar of salt (v. 26). There is no clear indication that she did so with the intent to take her own life.

3. Raymond R. Newell, "The Suicide Accounts in Josephus: A Form Critical Study," *Society of Biblical Literature 1982 Seminar Papers*, Kent Harold Richards, editor (Chico, Calif.: Scholars Press, 1982), 351–69. Newell cites other major studies of this subject and comments on several relevant passages in Rabbinic literature.

4. Ibid., 368.

5. An excellent discussion of the various texts and their importance is to be found in *Jesus Within Judaism* by James H. Charlesworth (New York: Doubleday, 1988), 90–98.

6. "The Letters of Ignatius" in *The Apostolic Fathers*, vol. I, critical edition by Kirsopp Lake in *The Loeb Classical Library* (London: W. Heinemann, and New

York: Macmillan, 1912–1913). Newell noted that the willingness to die for one's god among Jews was an indication of the growing belief in an afterlife, in Newell, "Josephus," 366.

7. *The Ecclesiastical History of Eusebius Pamphilus . . .*, translated by Christian Frederick Cruse (Grand Rapids: Baker Book House, 1955), 143.

8. Augustine, *City of God*, translated by Marcus Dods and others (New York: The Modern Library, 1950).

CHAPTER 2

1. Newell noted that when Rabbi Hanina b. Teradion was being martyred by fire, his executioner asked if, by helping the rabbi die sooner, he would enter the life to come. He was told yes, and after giving such help to the rabbi, threw himself into the fire. Both were declared by later writers to have been assigned to the world to come. (See 'Abod. Zar. 18a.) Newell then noted that a similar story might have lain behind the account of Judas's suicide, even if later Christian tradition did not generally understand the act as a self-initiated, salvific act of repentence, in Newell, "Josephus," 361–62.

2. John Donne, *Suicide (Biathanatos)*, transcribed and edited for modern readers by William A. Clebsch (Chico, Calif.: Scholars Press, 1983), 67–68.

3. Lloyd R. Bailey, *Biblical Perspectives on Death,* Overtures to Biblical Theology (Philadelphia: Fortress Press, 1979), 100.

4. Ibid.

5. There is no single word for suicide in the biblical languages. Only phrases are used. "Suicide" did not come into the English language until 1651. See Edwin S. Shneidman, " 'Suicide' and 'Suicidology,' " *Life-Threatening Behavior*, vol. 1, no. 4 (1971), 260–63.

6. This term is a basic element in Wogaman's system of ethics in J. Philip Wogaman, *A Christian Method of Moral Judgment*, 2d ed., (Philadelphia, Westminster Press, 1989).

7. Henry Romilly Fedden in his classic work, *Suicide: A Social and Historical Study* (London: Peter Davies, 1938), 70–85, gives a concise account of the stoic and epicurean arguments regarding suicide.

8. Ibid., 117.

9. Ibid., 91–92.

10. Ibid., 122–23.

11. Günther Bornkamm, *Paul*, translated by D.M.G. Stalker (London: Hodder and Stoughton, 1971), and Hans Conzelmann, *The Theology of Saint Luke*, translated by G. Buswell (London: Faber and Faber, 1960).

CHAPTER 3

1. Newell, "Josephus," 363.

2. John Knox, *New Oxford Annotated Bible*, edited by Herbert G. May and Bruce M. Metzger (New York: Oxford University Press, 1973), 1392.

3. Fedden, *Suicide*, 110.

4. John Donne, *Suicide*, 87. See also Elie Wiesel, *Five Biblical Portraits*.

5. Bailey, *Biblical Perspectives*, 91.
6. Ibid., 97.
7. Ibid., 101.

CHAPTER 4

1. Fedden, *Suicide*. Three helpful summaries are: Battin, *Ethical Issues*, 76-127, although the material is not presented chronologically; Marilyn J. Harran, "Suicide," in Mircea Eliade, editor, *The Encyclopedia of Religion*, vol. 14 (New York: Macmillan, 1986), 125-31, a broad look at other religions and cultures; and George Rosen, "History," in Seymour Perlin, editor, *A Handbook for The Study of Suicide* (New York: Oxford University Press, 1975), 3-29.

2. Jacques Pohier and Dietmar Mieth, *Suicide and the Right to Die*, x-xi.

3. Battin, *Ethical issues*, 33. Some hold that the best translation of the commandment is "Thou shalt not murder." See chapter 2, above.

4. Lactanius, *The Divine Institutes*, in *The Ante-Nicene Fathers*, vol. VII, edited by Alexander Roberts and James Donaldson (Grand Rapids: Eerdmans, 1899), 89.

5. In his "Table Talk" for April 7, 1532, he is reported to have said: "I don't share the opinion that suicides are certainly to be damned. My reason is that they do not wish to kill themselves but are overcome by the power of the devil. They are like a man who is murdered in the woods by a robber. However, this ought not to be taught to the common people, lest Satan be given an opportunity to cause slaughter. . . ." Martin Luther, "Table Talk," *Luther's Works*, edited and translated by Theodore G. Tappert (St. Louis: Concordia, 1967), vol. 15, 29. Luther also said that even a suicide came to death at an hour appointed by God. See his "Notes on Ecclesiastes," edited by Jaroslav Pelikan and Hilton C. Oswold, in *Luther's Works* (Philadelphia: Fortress Press, 1972), vol. 54, 51. Both the British philosopher David Hume and the cleric John Donne held that a suicide did not act outside of God's power to grant that act. For a concise discussion of the thoughts of these two men, see Battin, *Ethical Issues*, 49-52.

6. Donne, *Suicide (Biathanatos)*, The Third Part: Of the Law of God, 67-97.

7. Fedden, *Suicide*, 216.

8. John McManners, *Death and Enlightenment: Changing Attitudes to Death among Christians and Unbelievers in Eighteenth-Century France* (Oxford and New York: Oxford University Press, 1981), 428-29.

9. John Wesley, "Thoughts on Suicide," in *The Works of John Wesley*, vol. XIII, 3d ed. (Grand Rapids: Baker Book House, 1979), 481.

10. For a well-reasoned disagreement from a psychological/theological perspective, see Ronald Maris, "Rational Suicide: an Impoverished Self-Transformation," *Suicide and Life-Threatening Behavior* 12 (Spring, 1982): 4-16.

11. These six rabbinic tractates are included in *Babylonian Talmud* (London: Soncino Press, 1935-1959).

12. For a list of such occasions, see Feddin, *Suicide*, 147-49.

13. Dov I. Frimer, "Masada—In the Light of Halakah," *Tradition: A Journal of Orthodox Thought*, 12 (1971), 27-43. Among other works with important

interpretations of Saul see Louis Ginzberg, *The Legends of the Jews*, tr. by Henrietta Szold (Philadelphia: The Jewish Publications Society of America, 5714-1954); David M. Gunn, "The Fate of King Saul: An Interpretation of a Biblical Story," Sheffield: *Journal for the Study of the Old Testament Supplement Series* 14 (1980); and John A. Sanford, *King Saul, the Tragic Hero: a Study in Individuation* (New York: Paulist Press, 1985).

14. George B. Caird, *The Interpreter's Bible*, edited by George Arthur Buttrick and others, vol. 2 (New York and Nashville: Abingdon-Cokesbury Press, 1953), 1038–40. Caird does not include Abimelech, Samson, nor, apparently, the armor-bearer among suicides described in the Hebrew Bible.

15. See *Harper's Bible Dictionary*, Paul J. Achtemeier, ed. (San Francisco: Harper & Row, 1985), *Oxford Annotated Bible* (Oxford: Oxford University Press, 1962), *Jerome Biblical Commentary*, Raymond E. Brown, Joseph A. Fitzmyer, and Roland E. Murphy, eds. (Englewood Cliffs, N.J.: Prentice-Hall, 1968), *Chronicles One*, Jacob M. Myers, ed., Anchor Bible Series, vol. 12 (New York: Doubleday, 1965), and the *International Critical Commentary*, Ronald E. Clements and Matthew Black, eds. (Greenwood, S.C.: Attic Press, 1971) 190–94.

16. H.J. Rose, *Encyclopedia of Religion and Ethics*, vol. XII, edited by James Hastings (New York: Charles Scribner's Sons, 1928), 21–24.

17. John C. Schroeder, *The Interpreter's Bible*, vol. II, 1040, "He [Saul] had no will to live, because he could define living only in terms of his own existence. . . . Suicide is the ultimate of self-consciousness."

18. Norman Gottwald, *A Light to the Nations* (New York: Harper and Brothers, 1959), 191.

19. J.M. Myers, *Interpreter's Dictionary of the Bible*, vol. 2, edited by George Arthur Buttrick and others (New York and Nashville: Abingdon Press, 1962), 232. The opinion is given throughout the work, but expressed clearly here: "In the story of Saul, as in that of Job, we are at some distance from the innocuous God of the ethical absolutes: God can pour out his favour upon Israel, upon David, and even upon Saul; but he can also be unpredictably terrible, jealous of his own status, quick to anger and impatient of the complexities of human action and motivation," David M. Gunn, "The Fate of King Saul," 131.

20. Compare, among others, *The American Heritage Dictionary of the English Language*, edited by William Morris (Boston: Houghton Mifflin, 1980); *The Compact Edition of the Oxford English Dictionary* (New York: Oxford University Press, 1971); and *Webster's New International Dictionary of the English Language*, Second Edition (Springfield, Mass.: G and C Mirriam, 1936).

21. W. H. C. Frend, *Martyrdom and Persecution in the Early Church* (Oxford: Basil Blackwell, 1965).

22. T.C. Kane, "Suicide," *The New Catholic Encyclopedia*, vol. XIII (New York and elsewhere: McGraw-Hill, 1967), 781–83.

23. Marsha Norman, *'night, Mother* (New York: Hill and Wang, 1983). Among many other recent theatrical and film works are: Jarre Fees, Alice Liddle, and Larry Ketron, *Permanent Record* (Paramount Pictures, 1988); and Brian Clark, *Whose Life Is It, Anyway?* (New York: Dodd, Mead, 1978).

CHAPTER 5

1. Battin, *Ethical Issues*, 164.

2. Simeon was a fourth-century Syrian ascetic who earned sainthood by martyring himself through thirty-six years of self-initiated isolation from the evil world about him.

3. A. Alvarez,*The Savage God: A Study of Suicide* (New York: Random House, 1972), preface.

4. Joseph Laitin, "Ombudsman" column, *Washington Post*, Sunday, January 25, 1987, B6.

5. Jim Wall, "Combating Science on Death and Dying," *Christian Century* 101 (August 1–8, 1984), 731–32. Wall was writing partly in response to a well publicized statement by then governor of Colorado Richard D. Lamm that the terminally ill elderly have a "duty to die."

6. Shiela Graham, "Cabinet Will Study Ways to Control Husbands' Violence," *The Times* of London, Saturday, April 15, 1989, 5.

7. Betty Rollin, *Mother's Last Wish* (New York: Linden Press/Simon and Schuster, 1985).

8. See, for example, *Parade Magazine*, Sunday, January 29, 1989, 2.

9. Robert Graef, *Talking Blues* (London: Collins Harville, 1989).

10. Dietrich Bonhoeffer, *Ethics*, edited by Eberhard Bethge, translated by Neville Horton Smith (New York: Macmillan Paperback Edition, 1965), 168, 170.

11. For a particularly poignant personal account of such a situation see William A. Holmes, "Fifty Thousand Suicides a Year!" in *Sermons on Suicide*, 48–54.

12. In "A Paper Adopted by the 121st General Assembly and Commended to the Church for Study (Study Guide Included), 1981." Copies available from: Materials Distribution Service, 341 Ponce De Leon Avenue, Atlanta, Ga. 30365.

13. Ibid., 29.

14. The Westminster Shorter Catechism of 1647 is included in the Constitution of The Presbyterian Church (U.S.A.), Part I, The Book of Confessions. In Part II, Book of Order, however, the first of the "Historic Principles" includes the statement which allows members a certain freedom of conscience in this and other matters: ". . . we consider the rights of private judgment, in all matters that respect religion, as universal and unalienable. . . ."

15. See "Suicide: A Challenge to Ministry," *The Book of Resolutions of the United Methodist Church 1988* (Nashville: The United Methodist Publishing House, 1988), 317-22.

16. Bernard Zlotowitz, Ramie Arian, "The Value of Life: (The Reform Jewish View of Suicide)", Union of American Hebrew Congregations, 838 Fifth Avenue, New York, NY 10021.

17. Clemons, "Suicide and Christian Moral Judgment," *Christian Century*, 102, no. 16, May 8, 1985, 466–69. The criticism of not providing much "substance" and no "enlightenment" about what the Bible says on suicide appeared in the July 3-10, 1985 issue, 660.

18. Clemons, "How the Church Can Respond to the Suicide Crisis," *Response*, 1986, 22-23.

Annotated Bibliography

Alvarez, A. *The Savage God: A Study of Suicide.* New York: Random House, 1972. An overview of the personal struggles of a survivor to cope with a close relationship ended by suicide.

Battin, Margaret Pabst. *Ethical Issues in Suicide.* Englewood Cliffs, N.J.: Prentice-Hall, 1982. A thorough discussion of many topics posing personal and social questions, beginning with traditional religous and biblical views.

Clemons, James T., editor and contributor. *Perspectives on Suicide.* Louisville: The Westminster/John Knox Press, 1990. Up-to-date information and basic guidance on psychological, sociological, biblical, ethical, and pastoral care issues.

——, editor and contributor. *Sermons on Suicide.* Louisville: The Westminster/John Knox Press, 1989. Pastors and seminary professors offer a variety of biblical texts, personal illustrations, statistics, pastoral approaches, and ethical probings in thirteen sermons, most of which were not preached at funerals.

Department of Health and Human Serivces. Alcohol, Drug Abuse, and Mental Health Administration. 1989. *Report of the Secretary's Task Force on Youth Suicide.* Vol. 1, *Overview and Recommendations.* Vol. 2, *Risk Factors for Youth Suicide.* Vol. 3, *Prevention and Interventions in Youth Suicide.* Vol. 4, *Strategies for the Prevention of Youth Suicide.* Washington, D.C.: U.S. Government Printing Office, 1989. The result of four years of study by the nation's leaders in all the branches of suicidology of youth, the work includes articles on 50 topics, plus recommendations, summaries of National Conferences, and an inventory of DHHS activities in suicide prevention.

Fedden, Henry Romilly. *Suicide: A Social and Historical Study.* London: Peter Davies Limited, 1938. The classic work in the field. Philosophy, religious views, social attitudes and laws, case histories, literary depictions, and statistics. Basic for individuals and groups.

Grollman, Earl A. *Suicide: Prevention, Intervention, Postvention.* 2d ed. Boston: Beacon Press, 1988. A guide for understanding the phenomenon and for dealing with the tragedy at different stages, by a prominent rabbi.

Harran, Marilyn J. "Suicide," in *The Encyclopedia of Religion*. Edited by Mircea Eliade. Vol. 14, 125–31. New York: Collier Macmillan, 1987. A concise overview of suicide as treated by the religions of the world.

Hewett, John H. *After Suicide*. Philadelphia: Westminster Press, 1980. Help for those who survive and for those who seek to help them.

Klinefelder, Donald S. "The Mortality of Suicide," *Soundings* (Fall, 1984) 336–54. A philosophical treatment of some moral questions, helpful in grasping the complexities of suicide.

National Committee on Youth Suicide Prevention. *Young People in Crisis*. This film features Dr. Pamela Cantor, Lecturer on Psychiatry, Harvard Medical School, and Chair of the National Committee. Particularly helpful for parents and those who work with youth. Available from EXAR Communications, Inc., 267-B McClean Avenue, Staten Island, New York 10305.

Shneidman, Edwin. *Definition of Suicide*. New York: John Wiley and Sons, 1985. A leading suicidologist focuses on the necessity of proper definition for both accurate statistics and proper response, including the most effective prevention.

The United Methodist Church. *The Book of Resolutions*. Nashville: The United Methodist Publishing House, 1988. See "Suicide: A Challenge to Ministry," 317–22. An excellent example of what a church body can resolve to do after careful study by clergy and laity.